# Gratitude
# Marketing™

# Gratitude Marketing™

HOW YOU CAN CREATE

## clients for life

BY USING 33 SIMPLE SECRETS FROM
SUCCESSFUL FINANCIAL ADVISORS

*including the*
7 STEPS *of* IMPLEMENTATION

**MICHAEL F. SCIORTINO, SR.**

Published by Advantage, Charleston, South Carolina.
Member of Advantage Media Group.

ADVANTAGE is a registered trademark and the Advantage colophon is a trademark of Advantage Media Group, Inc.

Printed in the United States of America.

ISBN: 978-1-59932-619-1
LCCN: 2015947973

Book design by Megan Elger.

This publication is designed to provide accurate and authoritative information in regard to the subject matter covered. It is sold with the understanding that the publisher is not engaged in rendering legal, accounting, or other professional services. If legal advice or other expert assistance is required, the services of a competent professional person should be sought.

Advantage Media Group is proud to be a part of the Tree Neutral® program. Tree Neutral offsets the number of trees consumed in the production and printing of this book by taking proactive steps such as planting trees in direct proportion to the number of trees used to print books. To learn more about Tree Neutral, please visit **www.treeneutral.com**. To learn more about Advantage's commitment to being a responsible steward of the environment, please visit **www.advantagefamily.com/green**

Advantage Media Group is a publisher of business, self-improvement, and professional development books and online learning. We help entrepreneurs, business leaders, and professionals share their Stories, Passion, and Knowledge to help others Learn & Grow. Do you have a manuscript or book idea that you would like us to consider for publishing? Please visit **advantagefamily.com** or call **1.866.775.1696.**

The author is available for consulting, speaking and training engagements. He may be reached at:

 Mike@GratitudeMarketingBook.com

Gratitude Marketing
P.O. Box 424
Madisonville, La. 70447

www.linkedin.com/in/michaelsciortinosr

*I want to express my gratitude and love to the most significant person in my life, my high school sweetheart and wife, Mary, who has graciously and enthusiastically joined me in our magnificent journey. May we continue to work together to have a positive impact on others.*

*I love you!*

# TABLE OF CONTENTS

*First do what is necessary.*
*Then do what is possible,*
*and before long, you will find*
*yourself doing the impossible.*

—St. Francis of Assisi

# PREFACE

I would like to express my gratitude to, and encourage your active participation in, a very special charity, *Operation Gratitude*. This charity seeks to lift the spirits and meet the evolving needs of our active duty and veteran communities by providing opportunities for all Americans to express their appreciation to members of our military. Operation Gratitude annually sends 150,000+ care packages filled with food, hygiene products, entertainment, and handmade items, plus personal letters of support to soldiers, sailors, airmen, and marines deployed overseas and to veterans, new recruits, first responders, and wounded warriors.

Operation Gratitude started in March 2003. Over the years, this charity has implemented several additional care package programs in response to developing needs within the military community. In December 2013 the charity celebrated its *one millionth* care package.

Operation Gratitude continues its mission to our military to provide every one of us the opportunity to say thank you. I want to say thank you and express my gratitude to our military in an active and meaningful way. Therefore, a percentage of the proceeds from this book will go to Operation Gratitude.

If you would like to learn more about Operation Gratitude, please visit http//www.operationgratitude.com.

—Michael F. Sciortino Sr.

# INTRODUCTION

*People don't care how much you know until*
*they know how much you care.*

—THEODORE ROOSEVELT

Have you ever wondered what the most successful advisors in the country are doing to build their business? During my many years of traveling from coast to coast to work with successful financial advisors, I found there was a common turning point that led to their increased revenue—the realization that they needed to maintain more consistent communications with their clients. These advisors asked two important questions: How can I serve you? How can I contribute? They realized that the reason their clients did business with them was twofold: (1) they identified and solved their clients' problems, and (2) their solution gave their clients peace of mind. They recognized that the secret to success was making their clients feel good. And making your clients feel good is the foundation of Gratitude Marketing™, because while your clients might forget what you say, they will never forget how you made them feel.

*Gratitude is not only the greatest of virtues*
*but the parent of all others.*

—CICERO

A consistent program will provide your clients with the appreciated feeling they are seeking *and* produce dramatic results for you. Remember your clients already like you. If they didn't, they wouldn't be doing business with you. In their minds, you are someone they respect. Showing your gratitude for their business can only enhance your position.

Our business is dynamic and ever changing. Most advisors don't have the time to search for the best marketing strategies out there. We all like to talk about what our passion is, especially if sharing it enthusiastically means having a positive impact on many people. My passion has always been discovering creative and effective ways to market. My goal in writing this book is threefold:

1. I want to help you think differently about the role marketing can play in your success. The ideas I'll share with you have done one thing for me and the financial advisors who have used them—they have consistently produced results.

2. They say that the room for improvement is always the biggest room. I want to help you become more successful each and every day.

3. I want to give you a wealth of practical information organized in a user-friendly format. Think of this book as a recipe book and use just what you need at just the right time. My mission is to help you move your practice from first class to world class.

To be a world-class gratitude marketer you need to open your eyes to all the ideas around you. Wise men learn by experience, but wiser men learn from the experiences of others. I have studied the methods and activities of some of the most successful financial advisors in the business, and I will share the ideas I've collected with you. What you will learn will bring you closer to your clients. Upon completion of this book you will see that you can become more memorable and top of mind to your clients by investing in fun and engaging marketing activities. You will gain a broadened perspective of how other businesses are using marketing to gain your attention.

Back in the early 1980s I was in your shoes as an advisor. I can attest to the fact that the phone *can* indeed be dialed 300 times a day by starting early in the morning and working through the evening. It didn't take me long to realize that there were more creative and effective ways to build my business. I understand the struggles and challenges that you face. I know that what keeps you up at night is wondering how you'll acquire and retain clients. This book is for high achievers who want to take their businesses to the next level. But the strategies and ideas disclosed in this book can also be used by those advisors new to our industry to help jump-start their success by tapping into the accumulated experiences of the best advisors around. Either way, advisors who are willing to extend themselves above and beyond the average will distinguish themselves in their community through the use of Gratitude Marketing™.

Gratitude Marketing™ is all about what I refer to as FOCUS:

**F** — forever

**O** — offering

**C** — consistent

**U** — understanding

**S** — service

One thing is certain: to gain a competitive advantage, creative thought matters. Your clients receive over 3,000 marketing messages each day. So how can you stand out? If you are going to spend dollars on marketing, why not do it effectively and efficiently? Traditional marketing speaks *at* people. Gratitude Marketing™ engages and connects *with* people.

**Traditional marketing speaks *at* people. Gratitude Marketing™ engages and connects *with* people.**

My book will provide you with proven, practical, high-impact, fun, new ideas to turbo-charge your business by helping you crystallize your message. This will grow your business in a deliberate, measurable manner and better target and select the clients you want to work with. It will position you to attract customers, not pursue them. You'll discover that through Gratitude Marketing™, the more you give of yourself, the better marketer you'll become.

In fact, you could be just one idea away from dramatically increasing your income. Yes, one idea, successfully implemented, could transform your practice from first class to world class. You can customize these ideas to your practice. What I have found over the years is that those who have had the most success executing these concepts are those who, as the ideas were being presented to them, wrote down the names of clients they thought a particular idea would work best with. So I invite you to try doing that as you read through this book. By the end of the book, you will be able to comfortably answer the question, how can I apply these ideas in my business?

I will show you *how to increase client retention, how to increase referrals, and how to increase your revenue.* By simply showing regular and consistent interest in continually communicating with all of your clients and prospects, you'll enhance your chances of prospering. You'll discover proven ideas on how to separate your business from the competition by consistently acknowledging your clients, and you will learn how a change in your mind-set will produce proven results and increased revenue.

Most successful advisors achieved their success through effort and hard work. Through all the changes they encountered during their journey, they remained focused on the destination. Will Rogers said, "Even if you are on the right track, you'll get run over if you just sit there." He recognized the importance of continually moving forward. Socrates wrote, "The secret of change is to focus all of your energy, not on fighting the old, but on building the new." Each of these men was spot on.

I have always asked successful advisors what they thought made them so successful. Very often the answer is simply their mind-set. They have established a higher standard for themselves and their clients. They are driven not solely by fees and commissions but also by a sincere sense of responsibility and obligation to do the best job they can for their clients. It's no wonder that many of these successful advisors state that unsolicited referrals are the main growth drivers in their business. There is simply no substitute for authentic, personal, human-to-

**There is simply no substitute for authentic, personal, human-to-human relationships.**

human relationships. I will cover much more on referrals later in the book.

Successful advisors have learned that performing a series of regular daily actions with an unswerving outcome in mind is critical. They realized early on that there are no real failures, just learning experiences. They recognized that their thinking drives the size of their success and that you have to contribute before you can connect. They want to be extraordinary and accountable, and they live by the mantra that you only go through life once, so why not be the best? If you implement Gratitude Marketing™ today, what will it allow you to do in the future? Will you be building a sustainable business with the types of clients you want to serve? And how will you use your increased revenues? To fund your child's college? Pay for a wedding? Pay off your home? Or take that trip you've always dreamed of?

Years ago, I met an advisor who was a master of nurturing personal relationships. He taught me what it meant to communicate with my clients from the heart.

CT became a trusted friend, mentor, and role model to me. We all know people we love to be around because they inspire us and spread joy. CT was one of those special persons. Sure, he produced more business per square foot of office space than any advisor I had ever seen, but his workspace was also an extension of his home and his family.

I knew him as a man who was full of good old plain common sense, compassion, and humility for people, despite his having a physical handicap. Through his caring concern for his clients, he became one of the top producers in his firm. He believed there was no more important human quality than sharing with others and treating them with kindness and respect. At industry conferences, he would hold court at night after the sessions were completed. Whether advisors, wholesalers, or money managers, we sat captivated. He inspired us all and gave us hope that we too could succeed.

Every year, the first thing I would do when I got a new calendar was write in all my family birthdays and special events. Then I'd call CT to schedule our annual fishing trip to South Padre Island. Over the years, on those excursions, very little business was ever discussed. Instead, we talked about life and what mattered most. We discussed lessons to live by. Number one was family. With 58 years of marriage under his belt, he was a positive example—proof in action. Number two was fearlessness. He emphasized that I should not be afraid to take risks. He had learned more from his failures than his successes. "Try again," he would say in encouragement.

CT helped me train my eyes on the possibilities, not on the odds. Others were always the center of his focus. We talked often about fairness. He taught me generosity through his actions. He shared with me that he took a lot of losses by being fair because it was the right thing to do. I learned from him that success comes to those who approach this business with a love of their customers and the integrity to do right. He taught me to love my clients as family and to always express gratitude.

If you think about it, clients need two things from

**If you think about it, clients need two things from their advisor: someone they can trust, and someone they can count on.**

their advisor: someone they can trust and someone they can count on. CT was both.

This book will help you gain new clients, retain assets, and help you build that important bridge to the next generation—your clients' children. The strategies and ideas shared here will make your clients feel more appreciated and deepen your relationships with them. You'll find that Gratitude Marketing™ is not just a single event. It is a sound way of doing business. Does this work? Absolutely. Years ago, I asked one of my most successful advisors, "What's the secret behind the success that you've achieved?" His reply was very straightforward—"All I've ever done is follow my enthusiasm." He truly loved his business and the relationships he enjoyed with his clients. He thoroughly relished serving them and realized that the little things you do every day have a greater impact on others than you might think.

My objective with this book is to help and guide you as you implement the suggestions presented. I want to help thousands more advisors achieve what they want in life for themselves, their families, and their clients. You'll discover time-tested strategies that I've personally developed to help advisors grow their businesses. There's more opportunity in our business today than ever before. Through Gratitude Marketing™ I will show you how to increase the number of your clients, increase the average sales value per client appointment, and increase the frequency of client appointments. If you think about it, these are the only three ways in which you can grow your business. Let's get started.

# CHAPTER 1

# What is Gratitude Marketing™?

*In every person from the cradle to the grave
there is a deep craving to be appreciated.*

—WILLIAM JAMES

Where do you see your practice in five years, in ten years? What's your succession plan? One thing is certain, and that is, the more assets you amass, and more importantly, the more assets you retain, the greater the value of your practice. I've worked with advisors from almost every state in our country, and while investments are their primary business, I found the best advisors have also mastered marketing. Using demonstrated strategies, you too can master marketing, not just any type of marketing but Gratitude Marketing™.

What is Gratitude Marketing™? A couple of years ago, I hosted a dinner for financial advisors in the Sir John Templeton room of the Union League in Philadelphia. I jotted down a quote that was on the wall. "Unfortunately, too often people focus on the negatives and lose sight of the multitude of blessings that

surround us and the limitless potential that exists for the future."
And yes, that is a quote from Templeton.

At that moment, I was reminded that it doesn't hurt to step
back every once in a while and be grateful for what we have and
all the opportunities in front of us. This is the foundation of
Gratitude Marketing™. The number-one asset in your practice is
your client relationships, and you can use Gratitude Marketing™
to effectively maximize those relationships with your clients.
Remember, abundance multiplies when you show regular
and sincere appreciation.

**Remember, abundance multiplies when you show regular and sincere appreciation.**

Gratitude Marketing™
is a dynamic, client-centered
strategy primarily designed
to narrow your focus and
maximize the relationships
you have already cultivated. It's
about recognizing and developing more meaningful relationships with the clients you are
committed to for the long term, not just for one transaction. This
strategy expresses your commitment to providing caring solutions
to the changing needs of your clients *and* helps you build the
bridge to the next generation.

Gratitude Marketing™ taps into the wisdom of proven professionals who have used these cutting-edge, real-life ideas to build
their businesses. It's about employing the most effective marketing
to continually make a difference in your practice and a profound
difference in the lives of your clients as they progress through the
various stages of life.

Gratitude Marketing™ is a change in mind-set. It is a strategy in which your clients go from being sold something to being prescribed something. It allows you to go from just making money for your clients to making a meaningful difference in their lives.

*Webster's Dictionary* defines gratitude as the state of being grateful or thankful. And marketing is defined as the act of selling or purchasing in a market. What does *Wikipedia* say? It defines gratitude as a positive emotion or attitude arising from acknowledgment of a received benefit. So let's take a quick pop quiz. Which are the two most impactful words in the English language? The answer is *thank you.*

Each and every one of us longs for recognition and to hear these two words, which cut to the heart and allow you to connect in a powerful way. Gratitude opens our eyes to the richness of our relationships. But it isn't enough to just *feel* grateful. You have to *show* it. And that's where Gratitude Marketing™ comes in. It is a form of targeted marketing with applications in both mature and new practices. All our businesses are works in progress. Each day is a new beginning. People will forget what you *said*, people will forget what you *did*, but people will never forget how you made them *feel*. Gratitude Marketing™ is based on using ideas that keep your name in front of your clients so that you'll never have to hear your clients say, "I didn't know you did that," because they didn't think that a particular service was available from you.

The best financial advisors have found that more hours and harder work are not the answer. Often it's simply a matter of aiming at a higher market. These advisors have learned that you have to market yourself: who you are, what you are, what you do, and how you do it. Why? Because you get to choose whom you want to work with over the long term, and that matters a lot.

Why not plan and market to those you'd like to have a strong, long-term relationship with? In other words, why not only work with your ideal clients?

Are you a standout marketer? I'm not referring here just to your business experience or credentials. I'm referring to the way you stay top of mind with your clients. The most successful marketers I have worked with don't just market like everyone else in our industry. They look at other industries and ask, "How can I adapt that idea and use it in my business?"

Stop for a moment and think. In what ways have you been shown gratitude? Can any of these ideas be used in your business? What would it take for you to implement them? What impression will they make on your clients? Today many financial advisors base their value proposition on price and performance. But as fees are lowered, or as performance lags, asset retention becomes a real challenge. An alternative is to base your value proposition on a strong, nurtured, long-term relationship—a relationship focused on client trust. This is Gratitude Marketing™. It's a client-centric process that addresses the fact that clients want direct personal contact, and they want it on a regular basis.

**This is Gratitude Marketing™. It's a client-centric process that addresses the fact that clients want direct personal contact, and they want it on a regular basis.**

## HAVE YOU THANKED YOUR CLIENTS TODAY?

If not, you run the very real risk of other advisors courting your clients. It's a funny thing in life that, many times, we don't appreciate what we have until we lose it. Throughout time, people have always wanted to be appreciated, and they still do today. Clients are no different. Every day presents us with the opportunity to express gratitude through marketing.

## THE APPETITE FOR A SINCERE
## THANK YOU IS UNLIMITED

It's simple. If you want more business, start by thanking the people who already give you business. As an advisor, the words you use while communicating with your clients can enable you to connect in a more meaningful way. The other day, I ran across some notes from a conference I attended many years ago. I was struck by how this information still applies so well even today. Pay special attention to the meaning behind the words. The feelings they inspire are often more powerful than the words themselves. Your clients' subconscious mind recognizes and acts upon words that have been well thought out and that ignite their feelings.

**Here are the four powerful word combinations you can use:**

1. **Thank you.**

2. **Would you please?**

3. **What do you think?**

4. **I am proud of you.**

The common denominator is *you*. This is about *you*. Frequent use of the word *you* in your presentations and meetings allows you to establish a level of personal comfort and care for your clients. Your clients should walk away from a meeting convinced that you are concerned about them. As Mother Teresa said, "Kind words can be short and easy to speak, but their echoes are truly endless."

## GRATITUDE MARKETING™ IS ALL AROUND US!

Just about every industry practices Gratitude Marketing™. Once you complete this book, you will begin actively looking for additional ideas you can adapt and use in your business.

So who is the ultimate Gratitude Marketer? Envelope, please. The winner is...Southwest Airlines. That company gets it. It has the answer to this one question, which is, "What's the most important word in marketing?" *You* is the most important word in marketing. Always. On a recent Southwest Airlines flight, I was served my cup of coffee, and, as usual, I received a Southwest napkin.

FIGURE 1.1

On one side was a map of the United States and all the places the airline flies. But what struck me was the napkin's headline: **"We're America's largest domestic airline for one reason: You."**

This, indeed, is why Southwest is the largest. Again, that airline gets it. It goes out of its way to serve you, the customer. It also focuses its marketing on you, their customer. I have flown this airline for more than 25 years, and I have witnessed countless examples of world-class service and Gratitude Marketing™. From the ticket agents to the baggage handlers, from the flight attendants to the pilots, they all realize their number-one mission is to serve you, their customer. All members of this company understand that Southwest is a customer service company that also happens to be an airline.

As far as Southwest Airlines is concerned, I am just a customer, as you might be or have been, but because I fly a lot for business, I am a frequent customer, which has given me the opportunity to watch this airline's operations for years. Here's a personal example of Southwest's Gratitude Marketing™: Years ago, after traveling all week, I came home to find a message on my answering machine. It was from the customer relations department at Southwest Airlines. I called back and a pleasant voice on the other end said, "Hey, we wanted to call you. There's a game coming up in New Orleans and since you are our number-two traveler out of New Orleans, we would like to invite you to attend."

I said, "Great. What's that?"

The voice on the other end replied, "It's the Super Bowl."

I said, "Really?"

And the voice answered, "Yes. There's only one stipulation: you can't sell the tickets; you have to use them."

I said, "Great. I'll definitely use them." And I did go to the game with my wife. We live 40 miles outside New Orleans, so we drove into town, had a delicious brunch, went to a great game, and were back home at eleven o'clock.

Two weeks later, I was at a conference. I went up to a friend and said, "You are never going to guess what happened to me. Southwest Airlines called me and gave me two tickets to the Super Bowl because I was the number-two flier in the city of New Orleans."

He smiled and replied, "I have you beat. I got two tickets because I was the number-one flyer." What a fabulous example of Gratitude Marketing™!

Talking of successful gratitude marketers, Disney is a close second. When you are a guest at a Disney property, each time you pass through a security gate, you are greeted with, "Welcome home." This is a very heartwarming greeting. Another example of a premier gratitude marketer is TOMS Shoes. In a recent interview, Blake Mycoskie, the founder of TOMS shoes, commented that people connect with his company because buying a pair of TOMS shoes is like wearing a badge that says, "I did something for someone." Other firms are beginning to focus on Gratitude Marketing™, such as LATAM Airlines Group ("For *you*, it's business. For us, it's personal."); Fidelity ("We'll help you build a retirement life *you* want."); Hertz ("The benefits start even before *you* turn the key."); and Trump Hotels, ("Live the life.

**These days it's hard to find a service business that *hasn't* implemented Gratitude Marketing™ in one form or another.**

Most hotels give *you* a room. We give *you* the entire city."). Airline frequent flyer programs, hotel frequent user programs, and credit card reward programs are all examples of Gratitude Marketing™.

These days it's hard to find a service business that *hasn't* implemented Gratitude Marketing™ in one form or another. All of this is important to you, as a financial advisor, because these firms are all target-marketing our demographic and ideal client. Focusing on our gratitude reminds us of what we owe others and, perhaps, reminds us of our dependence on those around us.

> *Showing gratitude is one of the simplest yet most*
> *powerful things humans can do for each other.*
>
> —RANDY PAUSCH

For most advisors, the question is not whether you know how to show gratitude but whether you are doing it on a consistent basis and including it in your marketing. If this emphasis on marketing "for you" works for all these firms, I have a strong feeling that it will work for you as well. Try including it in your presentations: "Mr. and Mrs. Client, this is what this investment will mean to *you*." This will measurably increase your ability to connect with your clients.

Relationship capital isn't an asset; it's a privilege. Ultimately, what shapes the meaning of our lives is not what we have but what we give. If you can make it your goal to each day find a way to add value to your clients' lives, then you'll never have to worry about success. My hope is that you use the ideas and the methods in this book as a blueprint or road map for creating your own Gratitude Marketing™ plan to enhance and nurture client relationships. To be a world-class gratitude marketer—to be the very best—you must be a giver. Staying top of mind is critical to your long-term success. I will show you how to approach everything with an attitude of gratitude, consistently and consequentially. I will show you how to use Gratitude Marketing™ to define and differentiate your business. Gratitude Marketing™ will ensure that you deliver an unforgettable experience to your clients. The goal for each advisor using Gratitude Marketing™ should be to be able to claim, "The experience we provide is the best our clients will find, period."

# CHAPTER 2

# Why Use Gratitude Marketing™?

*Think of giving not as a duty but as a privilege.*

—JOHN D. ROCKEFELLER JR.

Today your clients have more distractions than ever before: telephones, e-mails, Twitter accounts, Facebook accounts. So how do you, as an advisor, stand out amid all the clutter?

The objective of most practices is to reach the most people and tell your story more effectively. But what if you already have a fantastic group of clients? The secret is to give them no reason to go elsewhere. And the way you do that is by creating and working with a "gratitude attitude." Continually ask yourself, how many more ways do I have to serve my clients? What other services can I present to them? When you approach your business in this way, it truly becomes a game changer. As Oliver Wendell Holmes observed, "Man's mind, once stretched by a new idea, never regains its original dimensions." That goes for your business too.

Think about this for a moment: Why is the Super Bowl so popular? Is it because of the actual game? Rarely. Many Super Bowls have been lopsided blowouts. The Super Bowl is extremely popular because the NFL has created an overall experience around it. There is the week's buildup to the game, full of activities for fans of all ages, and there's the anticipation each year of which company will produce the best commercial—the one that resonates with everyone. It is the full experience that makes the Super Bowl connect with so many fans.

Gratitude Marketing™ helps you to connect on a deeper level with your clients and to build bridges to the next generation, your clients' children. What I found is that your income leaps and your competitive edge increases when you move from selling products and services to offering solutions and experiences to your clients. The main question for you to consider from your clients' perspective is why your clients should choose to do business with you versus any other available option they have? The answer is simple. It's because of the caring experience you provide them.

**Gratitude Marketing™ helps you to connect on a deeper level with your clients and to build bridges to the next generation, your clients' children.**

*No person was ever honored for what he received but for what he gave.*

—Calvin Coolidge

Grambling State University football coach Eddie Robinson cared for every individual on his team, so much so that when they built the new stadium, they placed a huge marker at the entrance to Robinson Stadium.

The slogan read, "Where everybody is somebody." We should all aspire to such a legacy in our business and in our life. Gratitude Marketing™ builds a trust bond with your clients. When you integrate what you care about in your work, you ingratiate yourself to others. They'll also trust you more and feel better about the financial decisions you make together.

Gratitude Marketing™ is an ideal asset retention tool but is much more than that. It is designed to meet the needs of financial advisors and provide time-tested tools and resources to help them succeed in business.

The timing to implement Gratitude Marketing™ has never been better. The dynamics of financial advising have changed dramatically since 2008. Cold calling is dead thanks to no-call lists and cell phones. It's more expensive to advertise, with companies spending close to $1,200 per consumer ad in 2009 versus $107 in 1960. By age 65, your clients will have seen more than two million commercials, but on any given day, they can only remember two of them. Time spent on social media has grown by almost three times the overall Internet usage rate. So if your marketing is not effective, it's money wasted. But if done correctly, your return on marketing dollars spent to retain quality clients would be much less than the cost of acquiring new clients. Relationships matter more than ever before.

Our biggest challenge, as financial advisors, is to help clients examine their dreams and goals carefully to find the most suitable path for them. Every financial goal that your client will, ultimately, achieve depends on the day-to-day small steps they take under your guidance. Clients simply want relief from worry. They're desperately seeking a clear, disciplined, and decisive plan of action to move them from where they are today, point A, to where they want to be in the future, point B. Now, while we do live in a world of endless possibilities, oftentimes your clients' paths pass through adversity, volatility, obstacles, and disappointment. As they move along their paths, your role, as their financial advisor, is to step back and objectively assess their progress and, when necessary, make adjustments. After you've crafted the vision and laid out their paths, the vital ingredient for continued successful implementation is good, honest, open communication in both good markets and in bad.

It all boils down to three things that all your clients want: to know how you'll serve them, what to expect from you, and how you'll communicate with them.

This brings me to the six distinct reasons why Gratitude Marketing™ will work in your practice:

1. When clients experience kindness and generosity from your business, it makes them want to support you by way of cultivating referrals. What your clients say about you, your company, and the services you offer is ultimately more credible than anything you could say yourself.

2. Giving to others is the greatest gift you can give yourself. Studies reveal that when we help others, we release additional endorphins into our system that build our immune system and give us what researchers call a "helper's high." If you've ever served a meal at a homeless shelter or visited the elderly at a retirement community, you know what a wonderful feeling that is.

3. The cost of attracting a new customer is high. It's a lot cheaper to retain than to acquire clients. Gratitude

Marketing™ is simply a way to utilize strategies to extend existing relationships. By digging deeper and nurturing your relationships with your clients, you're more likely to retain them.

4. The number-one asset your business has is your client relationships. When you combine relationship-building ideas with consistent nurturing, you create *clients for life*. How many advisors have systems in place to regularly contact their clients? How effective are those systems? What you'll find as you go forward in this book are a number of ideas that will help you do just that on a consistent basis.

**When you combine relationship-building ideas with consistent nurturing, you create** *clients for life.*

5. A client relationship can become more valuable if you commit to systematic, reliable, and meaningful communication. Many clients lost money in 2008. So there's a loss of confidence and a hesitancy to stay the course. Studies show that if you have a good relationship with your clients, they're more likely to stay with you regardless of the short-term return. With asset retention being the top concern of financial firms, retaining clients now, as well as after an advisor retires, is a priority.

6. Any practice today is valued by its assets under management. An advisor who uses Gratitude

Marketing™ will have a higher retention of assets and create a more stable practice. It becomes an exit strategy. Your company will sell for more if you institute predictable marketing systems now that will remain in the business long after you exit. It is the most predictable route to increasing recurring income in your business—which, ultimately, is what determines the company's value.

My road to Gratitude Marketing™ began years ago when I started teaching adult continuing education courses on investing. What I discovered is that the people who actually came to the classes did so because the classes represented to them a very nonthreatening way—a very non-sales way—to learn how they needed to go forward.

By going in and presenting my information in a very conversational way, I found that people gravitated toward that approach versus what I call a traditional sales pitch. The course took place in a high school located in a very industrial area. There were a lot of manufacturing plants from which guys would retire in their mid-50s, and they would retire with a fairly generous retirement plan.

The reason why they took the course is because they were intimidated by big firms. But they weren't afraid to come down to the local high school to hear what somebody had to say.

After you spend several weeks with someone, for an hour at a time, you develop a rapport. Once I was able to sit down with one or two of them and do business with them, the word got out. The referrals started to generate. I then started to get them together as a group and do social outings.

My realization was that building relationships is really what it is all about; it's not about a single transaction. And Gratitude Marketing™ is all about that relationship.

If you pitch a product and that pitch is not a strike but a ball, they throw you out of the ballpark. On the other hand, if instead of pitching, you engage or connect, the client is more likely to give you a pass when there's volatility in performance. The epiphany for me was when I realized that my business's foundational relationship with clients enabled them to much better tolerate the occasional market volatility. By developing your clients' trust and by utilizing not just one idea in Gratitude Marketing™ but a number of ideas, you can nurture that relationship. That, to me, was the difference maker. That's what took me from being able to open five or ten accounts a month to being able to open 30 to 35 accounts a month on a regular basis.

Look at it as if it were a farming operation. What does a farmer do? A farmer goes out and plants a whole lot of seeds, and he hopes for a good harvest. He repeats this every season. Our business is no different. You have to constantly plant seeds, and what better way to do it than to make it fun, make it personal, make it seasonal, and make it mindful?

Gratitude Marketing™ is about staying top of mind in your community. It's about doing the things that matter. So let me ask you what you want people to think of when they hear your name. Are you the person who provides amazing guidance and enthusiastic encouragement as your clients move toward their goals? Do you provide simple solutions? Have you helped them make great memories with their family and friends? Do you use simple concrete examples to show them how they could take simple steps to become more successful? Are you always focused on their needs? Do you keep them centered not on what they've lost but on what they've gained? Do you always give them your best effort and a little bit more?

Ask yourself if your marketing is memorable, if it is producing results, and if you are providing an unforgettable experience to your clients.

The good news is that you can craft your marketing by the way you present yourself and conduct your business. Take your pick from the list of questions above and construct your firm's message. You are dealing daily with clients and prospects who have problems that are disrupting their lives. Build your business around the right message—one that projects your strengths and passions—and how you can apply that message to help them. Then stay open to the possibilities that Gratitude Marketing™ can provide.

Harvey Mackay believed "you can win more friends with your ears than with your mouth. People who feel like they're being listened to feel accepted and appreciated. They feel like they're being taken seriously and what they say really matters." Isn't that how we all want our clients to feel? Sure it is. Being known as the difference maker in your clients' lives is both satisfying and tremendously fulfilling. So leave your clients feeling good. If it matters to them, it's important to you too.

**So leave your clients feeling good. If it matters to them, it's important to you too.**

And the truth is that, in our business, if you aren't doing Gratitude Marketing™, other advisors are. Studies have found that clients need your constant appreciation, which is why advisors who practice Gratitude Marketing™ are growing at the pace they're growing. There's a trend toward giving in this country today. As we age, we move from just wanting to be successful to wanting to be significant. The act of giving creates a positive experience for you, as an advisor, and establishes a powerful level of emotional attachment between you and your client. Make gratitude a constant in your business as you acknowledge your clients and encourage ongoing active client appreciation from your staff. Success will follow.

# CHAPTER 3

# Gratitude Marketing™ Is a Team Sport

*Of all the attitudes we can change, surely the attitude of gratitude is the most important and by far the most life changing.*

—Zig Ziglar

About now you might be wondering where you will find the time to do all this marketing. The bigger question, really, is whether you can afford not to find the time.

Here are a few suggestions for you to consider.

Delegate within your office, which I know many of you do now. Hire a marketing person and pay that employee on a performance basis. Or simply outsource your marketing and pay your marketer on a performance basis. Today more folks own their own businesses, and they understand and embrace performance-based pay.

Now let's look at the numbers. When we do that, what we find is that the math is really simple. Would you be willing to invest a small amount of money in your business today in exchange for bigger recurring income over time? Once you calculate the lifetime value of a client or how much revenue that client will provide, you'll find that the relationship will be a very meaningful one in the long term.

But let's assume that you'll use your own staff. I'll start with this question: What sets your staff apart from the competition? It's probably the people. Ask yourself if they pour their heart and soul into their jobs. Do they make it happen? Do they have a true passion for serving your clients? Every point of contact you and your staff have with your clients is an opportunity to "wow" them. Creativity and collaboration are vital in Gratitude Marketing™.

Get your staff actively involved in your marketing. Are you rallying all your resources on your way to excellence? Are the members of your team regularly demonstrating a positive attitude toward your clients? Their attitude toward your clients goes a long way in determining your clients' attitude toward you.

Some of the most successful financial advisors I know do a great job of training their staff to embrace enthusiasm and show prospects what their life will be like after they become clients. Their thinking is rather basic. Treat prospects as clients.

As Norman Vincent Peale noted, "Any fact facing us is not as important as our attitude toward it, for that determines our success or failure."

What I've observed is that excellence is not a skill; it's an attitude—one that is practiced every day, and Gratitude Marketing™ is no different. Vince Lombardi believed that "the quality of a man's life is in direct proportion to his commitment to excellence, regardless of his chosen field of endeavor."

Recently, I ran across a quote by a well-known, retired CEO that exemplifies what successful advisors in our business display: "To me, excellence means being better than the best. Its achievement requires an introspective assessment of everything we do, say, or make and an honest inquiry; is it better than the best? If it is not, we will ask ourselves, 'What will it take?' And then rally the resources required to get there." That was said by Jack Welch, the ex-chairman of General Electric.

At a recent conference in Chicago, I was asked by an advisor what I would do to accelerate the growth of my business. My answer was that I would implement strategies that would help me stand out, stand apart, and stand above. This is one of the most fundamental founda-tions of many of the successful advisors we work with, and this is Gratitude Marketing™.

**My answer was that I would implement strategies that would help me stand out, stand apart, and stand above.**

How do you accomplish this? Well, as Henry Ford advised, "Nothing is particu-larly hard if you divide it into smaller jobs." What are these smaller jobs in your business? I would submit they are the day-to-day tasks that you and your staff perform. Are you creating a true human connection with your clients? What feel does your client have for the experience you create?

Think for a moment. How are clients or prospects greeted when they visit your office or when they call your office? Have you trained your staff to represent you in a certain way? Are their efforts or results monitored?

It's important to step back occasionally and ask what your clients will remember about the experience of working with you and your staff. Will it be the receptionist's ever-present smile? Will it be messages returned promptly and courteously? Will it be the staff's consistently upbeat attitude? Impress upon your staff the idea that what matters is how they make your clients feel. This reminds me of a story about a wise physician—when asked what the best medicine for humans was, he replied that it was care and love. He was then asked, "What if they don't work?" He smiled and answered, "Increase the dose."

What do you need to tweak in your practice before proceeding through the year? Is it the number of touches that you initiate with your best clients? Is it your client follow-up system? Is it your appointment scheduling process? Is it your planning and preparation, or is it simply phone etiquette training?

The best advisors I know are constantly asking these questions, testing, adjusting, and readjusting the finer and smallest details of the practice. They are consistently creating the habits that lead to a more productive practice. They realize, as Tom Hopkins pointed out, that "the number of times I succeed is in direct proportion to the number of times I can fail and keep on trying." So take action now.

When you have a moment, take each question one at a time and write down your goal for improvement. Break your goal into a series of steps beginning with those that are absurdly easy. Involve your staff in the process.

My question to you is what are you doing in your practice today to nurture an attitude of excellence? May I make a suggestion? At your next staff meeting, ask the staff who interact with your clients every day the following questions:

What can we do, as a firm, to bring even more benefit and value to the clients we already serve? (Answers may include communicating more frequently or maybe having more frequent face-to-face meetings.)

What are our clients' greatest needs that aren't being met by us today? Is there a complimentary service that we can offer? What have we done well and what are the implications of that?

How can we help our clients meet their needs? How much would it cost us to be able to provide these services? How can we extend ourselves to make our services available to anyone else in our clients' lives who might need our advice or help, such as friends, relatives, or coworkers?

Are we actively asking for referrals? How can we implement a formal customer referral system to bring in an immediate increase in clients and revenues? What events do we have planned for the upcoming year for our clients, and how can we be more meaningful in the lives of our clients? All of these questions can be addressed through Gratitude Marketing™.

Now that I've presented a number of questions to think about, brainstorm a little with your staff. You'll be amazed at what you learn and what ideas will surface as you explore these questions.

The point that I want to make here is that you don't have to do it all yourself.

Listen to your staff, because a lot of what you could do might come from what they hear in the day-to-day business. Clients often say, "Boy, wouldn't it be nice if the practice did this or did that?" and unless you solicit that feedback from your staff, you'll never know.

The more successful advisors I know are the ones who take an active interest in their staff. They even take it a step further. They'll put on a contest each month to reward employees who come up with ideas that produce the best results. They'll give them a dinner out or movie tickets or whatever it might be. And recognizing input from your staff will let them know you value their ideas to improve the practice. This cultivates creativity and allows them to savor the success of the firm.

Your main objective is to determine what your firm might do to enhance your clients' experiences. Let me take a restaurant as an example of how we could apply these lessons to your business.

**Your main objective is to determine what your firm might do to enhance your clients' experiences.**

**The way you create more value is by better understanding what's important to your clients now.**

Restaurants serve more than food. Restaurateurs put a lot of thought into the whole presentation of the meal. They plan every little detail. Restaurants actually don't serve up meals; they serve up experiences. The better the experience is, the more likely the customer is to return and maybe even bring back family and friends.

Your firm is no different. The way you create more value is by better understanding what's important to your clients now. It's amazing what happens when you step back for a moment and examine what you do now and what you can do even better. By listening to your clients and your staff, you'll be able to chart your course for success.

Every day, every week, and every month, we have an opportunity to leave a positive, lasting impression. Every client visit is an opportunity for your clients to spread the word about how well they are being treated and how different their experience with your firm is from what they may be accustomed to elsewhere. What a tremendous differentiator this can be for your business.

Perfect your client experience, and watch your revenues grow. Just don't do it alone. Involve your whole office.

# CHAPTER 4

# Making it Personal

*People may hear your words, but they feel your attitude.*

—John Maxwell

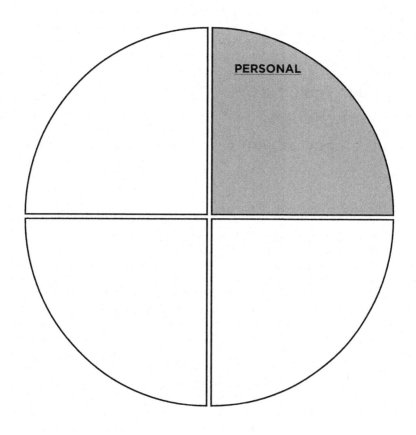

If you're going to spend dollars on marketing, why not do it effectively and efficiently? In the first two chapters, we examined the *what* and *why* of Gratitude Marketing™. Now let's look at the *how to* of successful strategies.

Like a menu with items spanning various price ranges, what you hold in your hands is a carefully selected group of proven, time-tested ideas you can use to take your practice to the next level and recognize your loyal clients. In the next four chapters, I will break down Gratitude Marketing™ into four areas: personal, fun, seasonal, and mindful. I'll be specific in giving you easy, actionable ideas to execute.

**Trust is earned through openness, integrity, and the consistency of your actions.**

Over the years, I've trained hundreds of financial advisors to use these ideas. They've obtained fast and proven results, and you can too. So let's begin by making it personal.

One of the key considerations your clients have prior to making a buying decision is trust. What influences whom they trust? One thing is certain. Trust is earned through openness, integrity, and the consistency of your actions. Gratitude Marketing™ is designed to create this type of consistency.

When I think of cultivating trust, I am reminded of the saying, "It's not a sprint; it's a marathon." Earning trust requires diligent effort over time. We've all heard that clients do business with people they like and trust. Why not make trust your competitive advantage?

When you have a relationship of trust with your clients, it enhances your ability to guide your clients to the actions they need to take to achieve their goals. However, like it or not, people have to be given the opportunity to come to their own feelings of trust at their own pace. That's where Gratitude Marketing™ comes in. Through a system of steady contacts over time, clients become more comfortable with your firm, and their trust strengthens.

How do we define trust? It's a firm belief, or confidence, in the honesty, integrity, and reliability of another person. Look at it like this:

**T** — total

**R** — respect

**U** — understanding

**S** — sincerity

**T** — thoughtfulness

As a professional, you garner trust by creating a belief system that enhances your clients' lives and gives them genuine hope. Most new clients are searching for a fresh direction. Trust tells them it's okay to follow your lead.

Gratitude Marketing™ nurtures this trust, which involves focusing on what's important to your client. Often what clients want is an advisor who can feel their pain and offer a prescription to fix it. In order to position yourself to take advantage of the greatest time ever to be in our business, you must focus on building this trust.

How do you cultivate trust?

1. Walk the walk and do what you say you'll do. If you do this one thing, you'll set yourself apart.

2. Always put the client's needs first. It's not just about the fees and the commissions. Do what's right, and the rest takes care of itself. Throughout the years, as I've traveled and worked with financial advisors, this one point has unfailingly separated the successful advisors from the struggling advisors.

3. Be accessible. Clients want to have the confidence that they can reach you when they need to. Make doing business with your firm easy, desirable, appealing, and fun.

4. Keep it simple. Clients trust whom and what they can understand. Make a habit of regular client communications that are easy to understand, easy to follow, and hard to forget. When I'm asked by an advisor, "What more can I be doing to build my business?" my reply is, "If you want to get what you've never had, you need to do what you've never done." However, in some cases, it may simply mean doing the things you've done before more consistently.

Trust is based on personal relationships. The most precious gift clients can bestow on you is trust. When they give you their trust, they have forged a partnership with you; it's personal. They believe in you. Making it personal is not hard to do, but it does require creating a measurable system in order to do it regularly. It means always making your clients feel special. So let's start with the first idea to make it personal.

# #1 RECOGNIZE YOUR CLIENTS' BIG DAYS

Nothing is more personal than your client's birthday or anniversary. Remember and acknowledge those big days in your client's life. Sure, you may have heard of this idea, but how many of you are actually implementing it?

It all starts with gathering the information. One advisor put out a card, like the one in Figure 4.1, in the reception area. How many of you have already filled out a card like this when visiting your doctor or dentist?

FIGURE 4.1

How impactful can the simple act of sending out a card to your clients on their birthday or anniversary be? Very impactful. If you don't believe me, let me share a story from my childhood with you. My mom and I had birthdays one day apart. Every year, she would receive a birthday card from the agent from whom my dad had purchased a life insurance policy for her. For one reason or another, my insurance was with the same company but with a different agent. In any case, I never received a card. Do you think I still have my insurance with that company today?

It's the little things that keep you anchored. Acknowledging your clients' significant dates will differentiate you from others. It's just human nature to remember those who remember you. To this day, I pay special attention when an advisor utilizes this simple idea because I realize its potential long-term impact. So make it a habit to make a client's day every day but, especially, on the big days.

## MESSAGE IN A MAILBOX

Direct mail continues to be used successfully today in many businesses. Here's a statistic that may surprise you: according to the Epsilon 2012 Channel Preference Study, 73 percent of US consumers and 67 percent of Canadian consumers said they preferred direct mail for brand communications because they could read the information at their convenience. Because everyone else just e-mails today, using direct mail can be a huge differentiator for you.

According to the US Post Office, a typical American household, these days, waits nearly two months before a personal letter shows up in the mail. When did the popularity of note writing end? Have we just identified an opportunity?

You've heard me say that the two most impactful words in the English language are *thank you*. Early in the chapter, I stated that trust is based on personal relationships. Thank-you notes and personal notes or letters build those relationships, which are the cornerstone of your business. Admit it. When you go out to the mailbox and find a personal letter or a handwritten note that you didn't expect, doesn't that lift your spirits and put a smile on your face? How many of you have actually sat down and written a letter or note to your clients to thank them for their business and tell them how important they are to you? These are the little difference makers. I know this requires discipline. Management guru Peter Drucker attributed much of his success in business to the fact that he sent out 12 thank-you cards every day.

Leo Buscaglia said, "Too often we underestimate the power of a touch, a smile, a kind word, a listening ear, an honest compliment, or the smallest act of caring, all of which have the potential to turn a life around." How do you find someone who needs encouragement? Look around you at home, at work, or wherever you are, and you will find people who are in need of encouragement. Here is the greatest news! Encouraging someone is easy. It can be done by anyone, anytime, anywhere. *Imagine the ripple effect if you encouraged three people today!*

**Imagine the ripple effect if you encouraged three people today!**

Be the voice of encouragement. Encouragement can pick someone up more quickly than a strong cup of coffee. Make no mistake; the success that takes place in the lives of your clients can start with your sincere encouragement.

Your encouragement sparks hope. I have heard it said that encouragement is the engine on which hope runs. If there is hope in the future, there is power in the present.

Your encouragement sparks action. Showing that you believe in your clients can make all the difference in whether or not they accomplish what they set out to do. Action supersedes everything.

Your encouragement sparks persistence. It's harder to give up on something when someone is rooting you on.

Let me suggest that you write three personal notes a day. With all the clutter of countless daily e-mails, this is a great way to reach out, differentiate yourself, and demonstrate to people that you felt they were important enough to take the time to write them a personal note. Do the math. Three notes a day times five days a week equals 15 notes a week. Allow four weeks off throughout the year, and you have 15 notes times 48 weeks, which means you have 720 chances a year to nurture relationships. Writing from the heart in a genuine, sincere way will enhance your connections. Notes and letters are expressions of gratitude and praise that many people hold on to for years. Nothing compares to a handwritten note from one human being to another. Financial advisors who send thank-you notes are thought of as gracious and well mannered. Since few regularly practice this lost art, those who do position themselves ahead of the competition.

 ## REASSURANCE LETTER

Our clients' peace of mind is very important. As humans, we all want to feel that our decisions are justifiable, prudent, and sound. How many of you send a client a reassurance letter within a week of their becoming your client? In our business, a favorable outcome may be a comfortable retirement, college education for our children and grandchildren, protection for our loved ones in case of disability or death, a well-funded emergency fund, or other specific goals. These are all long-term outcomes.

Today there's more focus on the moment and on disruptive events than on the long-term needs of families. We need to help our clients not to be victimized by short-term circumstances but, rather, to use these events as springboards for long-term wealth accumulation. We need to help our clients stay the course.

In the same way that a good teacher challenges and guides her students, this requires constant nurturing. These outcomes become more real and important to our clients if they can visualize the end result. If you can help your clients clearly see what the future may hold, they will have a much better idea of how to prepare for it. They will have a great deal more confidence as you move forward and the added courage to weather any short-term adversity. This will enable them to reach forward to achieve the vision of their future. As Zig Ziglar said, "A compelling dream will generate the obedience to push past our fears."

Experience in this business has taught me that a vital key to success is to help our clients discipline themselves to do what they *need* to do so that, at a later time in the future, they can do what they *want* to do. It is these decisions, not our circumstances, that determine long-term quality of life.

The four components of a great reassurance letter are:

1. A statement of appreciation or a simple thank you

2. An emphasis on reassurance

3. A re-emphasis on the value of your company

4. A reinforcement of the client's buying decision

Use this letter as another opportunity to solidify your personal relationship by connecting to what your clients have a deep interest in. Relate their accomplishment to their hobbies and passions. Focus on how you can help make their lives better. Show them specifically how they can benefit from the information you're sending. Never assume that they'll just automatically make the connection.

## #4 ONE CALL CAN CHANGE IT ALL

Set aside time each day to call three clients, just call to say hi and check in and be fully present in that conversation. Zig Ziglar stressed that "you never know when a moment and a few sincere words can have an impact on a life."

You're probably thinking, "Where will I find the time to do this?" Simply put, it requires you to exercise self-control. Oftentimes, the challenges or problems we face force us to grow and become more capable in our practices.

An astute mentor I had early on would reiterate to me that if I didn't act, something significant wouldn't happen. How right he was. Over the years, I've realized that I needed to discipline myself to make these calls. Why? Because your unwavering encouragement fuels your clients' hopes of achieving their goals. Your role is to put in place the positive steps to make the hoped-for results a reality. As an advisor, you have a tremendous platform to deliver a life-changing impact. Years from now, thanks to your guidance, your clients will be able to say, "I'm glad I did" versus "I wish I had." You can inspire your clients by presenting them with a practical and attainable positive vision for their future. With your help, your clients' compelling dreams will generate the discipline they need to push past their fears and reach their goals.

I have found there are two words, which if they're used regularly in your calls with your clients or prospects, can provide incredible growth in your practice. These two words help you to see things clearly from your clients' frame of reference. They help your clients reveal who they really are.

---

Ready for them?

*Tell me.*

---

Tell me about *you*: your hopes, dreams, goals, past experiences, successes and failures, likes and dislikes. Tell me about what you want and need. Tell me your *why*.

These two words are powerful. Face it: people are interested in themselves. They do business with those who take a sincere interest in them and listen to what they're saying they want and need. After listening to their clients, the successful financial advisors we work with are able to present only those key benefits of a solution that are of real importance to the client. This eliminates the clutter that occurs when too much information is presented and no decision can be reached on a course of action. This also gives you an opportunity to share with your clients what your company stands for and how such values will benefit them. Your path to greater success in client relationships begins with understanding and respecting how your clients view life.

Years ago, when I was just starting out in the business, I used to continually listen to recordings by successful sales trainers any chance I could. It was invaluable to hear stories about how these coaches handle all aspects of the selling process.

One morning, I was driving down the road on the way to an appointment, listening to the master of sales, J. Douglas Edwards, talk about the importance of active listening. All of a sudden he yelled out, "Shut up! Shut up!" This was followed by dead silence. He had made a point that, to this day, I've never forgotten. Once you've made your presentation, you need to sit back and listen to the client's response. You may feel that you're waiting an interminably long time, but the operative word here is *listen*. In this case, Edwards was trying to emphasize that when your clients finally do respond, they will tell you how you can help them solve their problems. A wise mentor told me, years ago, "If you want to be successful as an advisor, just remember there's a reason why you have two ears and one mouth." He went on to explain that what most clients need is a good listening to; they long for an advisor to see their world through their eyes by listening—really listening. Be prepared to listen, and listen to be prepared.

**Be prepared to listen, and listen to be prepared.**

Mastery is achieved when you refine the ability to consistently see situations the same way or from the same point of view as your clients do. *You* make it personal. As Henry Ford advised, "If there is any one secret of success, it lies in the ability to get the other person's point of view and see things from that person's angle, as well as from your own."

In order to improve your listening skills so that you may build stronger, longer lasting relationships, here are four steps to follow:

Step 1: Share your sincere insights and encourage your clients to share their goals, dreams, feelings, and frustrations. This will help you zero in on their true needs.

Step 2: Make a habit of being present, and give your clients your full, undivided attention. For this moment, block out all distractions and focus solely on them.

Step 3: Make your clients feel comfortable with sharing their thoughts openly and honestly. Treat this conversation as if you were visiting with an old friend.

Step 4: Once your clients finish talking, acknowledge what you heard without passing judgment. This will enable you to make sure everyone is clear on what the needs are prior to your making a recommendation.

Knowing and understanding your clients' frame of reference will enable you to more accurately identify what your clients really want and how you can provide it. It serves as the foundation for the fresh perspective that you can bring to help them reach their goals. It positions you as the solution for each client. So tell me, can it get any better? You have the potential to build a significant business that can have a positive impact on millions of clients' lives. All it takes are regular, focused calls—simple phone calls. If you connect, you never know what will come up. By asking the right questions, it's likely that things will arise that you can address. Understanding your clients and prospects on a more personal level will enable you to serve them better today. Yes, today is your day. Not yesterday, not tomorrow, but today. You have 86,400 seconds to make an impact today.

In the end, what clients really need is an advisor who, after asking all the tough questions, can construct the right portfolio for them. They need an advisor who can provide consistency while protecting them from catastrophic loss. They need an advisor who instills confidence in their choices and provides them with peace of mind. They need an advisor they feel comfortable talking to, as they would with an old friend. Are you that advisor? You can be, starting today. Just pick up the phone.

*Thankfulness is the beginning of gratitude. Gratitude is the completion of thankfulness. Thankfulness may consist merely of words. Gratitude is shown in acts."*

—HENRY FREDERIC AMIEL

## #5 THE TRUE VALUE OF A ONE-CENT STAMP

Examples of Gratitude Marketing™ are all around us. The other day, I received the card pictured here, from an advisor with whom I had worked many years ago.

FIGURE 4.2

On the surface, it appears to be a normal greeting card. However, inside is the following note, along with ten one-cent stamps. The note reads, "As you may be aware, the price of postage was recently increased by one cent. Do you have some older stamps sitting in a drawer, waiting until you can get to the post office to buy some additional postage? Well, [advisor's name] and [firm name] would like to help. We've enclosed some one-cent postage stamps.

Hopefully, we have saved you some time that will be worth more than the value of the stamps we are sending. From the beginning of our firm, we have believed that we were in business to help our clients reach their personal financial goals. We constantly work on strengthening, refining, and improving our services to benefit you, our client. If there is anything we can do to help, please contact us [advisor's tel. no.], fax us [advisor's fax no.], or e-mail us [advisor's e-mail]. You may also visit us at [advisor's company web address]." When her clients opened this card, did her message stand out? Did it illustrate her level of caring for her clients? Absolutely. She illustrated it well in a clever, professional, and—most importantly—unexpected way. How can you use your creative thinking to implement a similar idea? Go ahead. Make it personal.

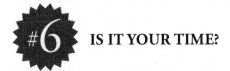 **IS IT YOUR TIME?**

Throughout my years of travel, advisors have frequently asked me what they can do if they've met with their prospects, listened to their needs, and presented a recommendation, and the prospects still haven't become clients.

Many times, advisors take all the necessary steps to convert prospects into clients, but the timing is simply not right. Often, situations and events in prospective clients' lives are so important to them that they just can't make the decision to move forward with the advisor.

If this happens to you, send your prospects a little clock with a short note that reads, "Isn't it time we moved forward implementing your plans for a comfortable retirement?"—or whatever else is their most compelling goal. As simple as it sounds, a creative idea like this can be the spark to action. Sometimes, it arrives at just the right time.

 ## ARE YOU A CONNECTOR?

What do you do with all the business cards you accumulate in the normal course of your daily life? Do you throw them in a drawer in your office, or do you save them and jot down the powerful connection points you may have learned when you met and spoke with those who gave you their card?

I know one particular advisor who has mastered the art of connecting. He goes out of his way to help everyone he meets and has for years. He's always looking to connect others, whether it's through business, sports, hobbies, or other interests. His mind-set is clear. Every time he meets someone he asks, "What can I learn from this person? How might I best help this person?" This advisor realizes that the more he communicates from the heart and to the heart of the relationship, the deeper the connection.

Over time, he has connected more people than anyone else I know, and his network and business has grown stronger and stronger as a result. As does a farmer who plants seeds now for the harvest later, he nurtures relationships.

Are you doing everything you can to make introductions—to connect people? This willingness to give of yourself without asking for anything in return is another subtle way to practice Gratitude Marketing™. A small investment of time will go a long way toward solidifying your relationships. Today's technology has provided you with an invaluable tool called LinkedIn. Are you utilizing it to open doors for others? Since relationships are the key to lasting success, think about how LinkedIn might help you and your clients or prospects.

## THE LAGNIAPPE: YOUR FEEDBACK PLEASE

(**Author's Note:** Down in Louisiana we're famous for "lagniappe." Lagniappe is a small gift given to a customer by a merchant at the time of purchase. It's something given or obtained gratuitously, or by good measure, such as the 13th donut when you buy a dozen. Here's my lagniappe, or bonus idea, for you.)

I'm always on the lookout for standout examples of Gratitude Marketing™. On a recent trip out West, when I was at a restaurant, I picked up a comment card that proved, on further inspection, to be an awesome example of Gratitude Marketing™.

Thanks for giving us the opportunity to serve you. We hope that we have met your expectations. If you have any concerns or have any suggestions to improve our service, please don't hesitate to let me know directly at: johnlong@me.com

JOHN LONG
*owner/chef*

## BE OUR FACEBOOK FAN: CAFE

ADDRESS | CITY, STATE | PHONE NUMBER | WEBSITE

FIGURE 4.3

Let's examine why. On one side of the card, the restaurant simply says thank you for choosing that restaurant. On the other side, the restaurant, once again, thanks customers for the opportunity to serve them and graciously solicits feedback and suggestions for improvements. It invites customers to visit its website and become Facebook fans.

This simple four-by-six card captures the essence of Gratitude Marketing™. You can design and adapt a similar approach for your clients. This simple accountability tool helps this restaurant identify ways in which it can improve and constantly grow, not to mention solidifying relationships with its patrons.

So keep your eyes open. You never know when or where the next terrific idea will appear that you can use in your practice.

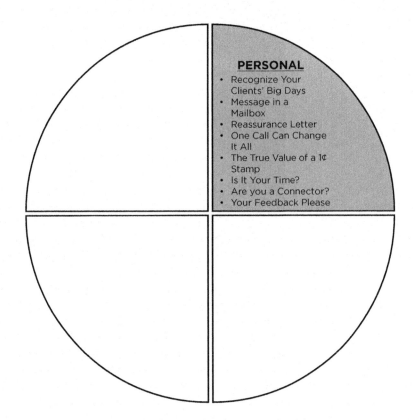

## MAKING IT PERSONAL RECAP

So how will *you* make it personal? Relationships are the hub that holds your business together. Your business is all about being connected in relationships with your clients. In this chapter, our focus was very simple: (1) how can you create deeper, more personal relationships, and (2) with whom do you want to create those relationships, in addition to your clients?

Thinking is the most highly paid profession. Pause now. Take a moment and journal your answers to the above two questions. This will help you stay laser focused as you begin to implement Gratitude Marketing™.

# CHAPTER 5

# Making it Fun

*You don't build it for yourself. You know what*
*the people want and you build it for them.*

—WALT DISNEY

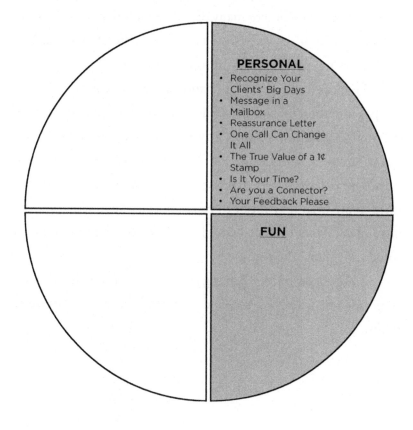

**PERSONAL**
- Recognize Your Clients' Big Days
- Message in a Mailbox
- Reassurance Letter
- One Call Can Change It All
- The True Value of a 1¢ Stamp
- Is It Your Time?
- Are you a Connector?
- Your Feedback Please

**FUN**

When we talk about fun, who better to lead the way than Walt Disney? Walt refined and mastered the art of Gratitude Marketing™. To this day, the Disney company is still about creating that magical experience for you, its customer.

Are you ready to take your practice and your life to the next level? Would you like to have fun doing it?

This chapter will help you focus on creating fun experiences for your clients. In all likelihood, you'll be doing something for your clients that your competitors are not. And you'll deliver such an unbelievable experience that your clients will fall in love with you and become clients for life.

I've yet to meet anyone who doesn't enjoy a little fun. Your clients are no different. For many of your clients, financial decisions are stressful, or at the very least, all business. But all work and no play makes for a lifeless relationship.

The ideas featured in this chapter are positive proof that you can pay attention to what your clients enjoy doing and craft a fun experience around that. And why not? Your clients want to feel special, respected, and cared for. Your clients are dear and valued friends who have put their trust in you. Reciprocate by letting them know what they mean to you on a consistent basis. You can nurture your client relationships by simply creating fun points of connection along the way.

As Zig Ziglar put it, "Among the things you can give and still keep are your word, a smile, and a grateful heart." So let's make it fun.

 LUNCH IT IS

Years ago, I worked with an advisor who used a very basic idea to perfection. He called it the birthday lunch idea. It's actually a brilliant extension of the birthday card idea discussed in the previous chapter.

Through the years, as this advisor brought on new clients, he would log them into his monthly birthday calendar. His thought was that by doing this one thing, he was creating a way to recognize the trust his clients had placed in him while, at the same time, nurturing referrals.

Here's how he executed this idea. Each month, he would call his clients who were celebrating a birthday in the upcoming month and invite them to lunch, encouraging them to bring three of their friends along. What client would not respond to such warmth and gratitude? If you want the heart to prompt the mind to do what logic points to, a warm, caring attitude is vital.

Abraham Maslow recognized this when he said, "The fact is that people are good. Give people affection and security, and they will give affection and be secure in their feelings and behavior."

What do you think executing this strategy did for the growth of his business, as well as for his client retention? It was not unusual for his clients to invite the same three friends to join them for lunch from year to year. This allowed the advisor the opportunity to get to know the friends prior to taking them on as clients. Once the friends became clients, he invited them to lunch on their birthdays with the same stipulation that they bring three of their friends along. Each year, as the number of candles increased, so did the fond memories.

Years ago, Dale Carnegie summed it up when he said, "You have it easily in your power to increase the sum total of this world's happiness now. How? By giving a few words of sincere appreciation to someone who's lonely. Perhaps you will forget tomorrow the kind words you say today, but your clients may cherish them over a lifetime." Judging from the success this advisor has enjoyed by using this one idea, truer words were never spoken.

*Wherever there is a human being, there is an opportunity for kindness.*

—SENECA

## BINGO AND BARBEQUE

When I sit down with top advisors, one of my favorite questions is "What strategies have you tried to improve or build your practice that did or didn't work?" This next idea is so simple you'll immediately start thinking about how to implement it.

I once worked with a very successful advisor who was located in a small southern town. Every year, he would invite me to what he called a client outing. After participating in these outings with him for a couple of years, I realized it really wasn't about the presentations we would give. Instead, it was about connecting in a fun, sociable setting while solidifying and initiating relationships. It was all about enjoying good barbeque together outside on a beautiful day.

FIGURE 5.1

Since this was a small town, everyone looked forward to this event every year. It was a conscious effort on his part to thank his clients for their business. He encouraged them to bring friends along, to have a great time, and indeed, a good time was had by all, including the advisor.

He would call out the bingo numbers during the bingo game. He would have raffle drawings throughout the event. He truly got more joy out of giving to others, and he put a good deal of thought, each year, into how he could enhance the previous year's fun. He never ceased to amaze me. He simply wanted to be the *last*

**He simply wanted to be the *last* financial advisor these clients would ever have, and he valued and cherished those relationships.**

financial advisor these clients would ever have, and he valued and cherished those relationships.

I have found that advisors who have a heart full of gratitude tend to be more positive, creative, and innovative. They also tend to socialize better, which makes them infinitely more successful over the years. This is why giving is so important. It goes beyond success. It involves caring.

As Adam Smith said, "The sentiment which most immediately and directly prompts us to reward is gratitude."

## #3 ANYONE FOR FASHION AND FINANCE?

I encourage advisors to form a strategic alliance with a business that already has relationships with clients who could become those

you're invited...

**FASHION
& FINANCE**
LUNCHEON

FIGURE 5.2

advisors' prospects. In one particular case, with the content that we wanted to present, the logical choice was the best women's clothing store in town.

The idea was to create an event—a luncheon—that combined the clients of both the advisor and the clothing store. Invitations were sent out to the two client groups. This was an excellent opportunity for both businesses to increase their visibility. It also enhanced their implied credibility. The financial advisor would make a presentation on women and investing while the women's store would have models show their latest clothing line. Might this idea also work with other businesses? What about a jewelry store?

Take a moment now and write down three businesses in your community that you can approach with this idea. Contact them and join efforts to create a memorable event. These joint ventures allow for cost and resource sharing. It is a true win/win for the advisor and the other business.

A side note here: The most common reaction I get to this idea is from the advisor who says, "You mean I've got to get up and speak? But I'm not a good speaker. I can't make a presentation in front of a crowd." Well, it's been said that luck is where preparation and opportunity intersect, so why not adequately prepare?

Have you ever attended a Broadway play? If so, you're familiar with the quality of these productions. What you may not appreciate are the hours and hours of preparation and practice that go into putting on the production. This is a proven formula for success.

Early on in my career I asked a successful advisor how he became such an accomplished speaker. His solution was simple. Prior to the evening of the seminar, it was not uncommon for him to deliver his presentation numerous times to an audience of one: his mirror. That enabled him to work out the proper pauses and correct voice inflections and to practice necessary mannerisms to connect with his audience. It also allowed him to become increasingly comfortable with the presentation and enabled him to anticipate the points that would prompt questions from the audience.

By showing up at the seminar well rested, relaxed, and confident, he was able to communicate his topics to his audience in a deliberate and understandable way. As Plato wrote, "The first and best victory is to conquer self." Once you can do this, you will be able to present with a clear mind that will be open to all the possibilities and opportunities around you.

If you really want to see your business explode, take the time to prepare a presentation on a topic you're passionate about. The famous golfer Gary Player summed it up perfectly when he said, "The harder you work, the luckier you get." How true.

 ANNUAL PARTY

How can you create a memorable client experience? Let's start with turning your *shoulds* into *musts*.

Over the years, I've heard them all. "I should put on a seminar. I should call three to five clients per day. I should mail three personal notes a day. I should plan my next memorable client event."

Now let's try that again. In order to achieve the results that you want in your practice, say this instead, "I *must* put on that seminar. I *must* call three to five clients per day." These are your opportunities to show your clients your appreciation and gratitude.

One of the secrets successful financial advisors have shared with me over the years is that many of their most effective ideas are not new. They've modeled their actions after other successful advisors. When you discover concepts used by others, you are, in effect, compressing decades of learning into days. That's working smart. One idea that I have taken from a successful advisor is an annual party in a local park. Here's how it works:

Every year, this advisor invites his clients and friends, along with all the leaders and movers and shakers in the community, to an annual party in the park. At the event, clients are served a buffet and entertained by a three-piece band. High school students, dressed in khaki pants and shirts bearing the advisor's company logo, serve guests. This builds goodwill by offering students much-needed service hours.

The annual party will help you expand your practice by creating a memorable client experience. So go ahead and start planning an event that is fun, something people want to do, and something that will allow you to stand out from the crowd. What are you waiting for? As W. Clement Stone pointed out, "Thinking will not overcome fear, but action will." Make it fun!

 **GOLF ANYONE?**

Through the years, I've played in my share of golf tournaments with advisors and their clients. We've sponsored putting contests, hole-in-one contests, closest-to-the-pin contests, and longest-drive contests. You name it; we've sponsored it.

I'd like to share with you an idea that is a little bit different. Instead of a golf tournament, golf clinics are set up for clients and prospects. The rationale is that in order to get busy executives away from the office, you need to appeal to their passion for golf.

I worked with advisors and their clients to organize such a clinic. We met with the golf pro at a local club to set up a series of clinics for eight golfers at a time. Over a three-month period, we scheduled different groups of eight every two weeks. The numbers were simple. Over three months, the advisor hosted six clinics of eight and reached a total of 48 clients and prospects.

The golf pro loved it because it created revenue for him and his club. It gave him an opportunity to showcase his expertise, which increased the potential for additional lessons. And it gave him a chance to work with new people who might become members of his club.

To recreate this idea for your clients, first, schedule the date of the six clinics. Then start calling your clients to fill the six clinics. An unanticipated benefit might be the occasional warm referral as clients ask if they can bring a friend.

The clinic is conducted by the golf pro and begins at 5:00 p.m. and lasts for an hour. It is followed by a brief 20–30-minute presentation by you on a timely topic of interest. Then cocktails and hors d'oeuvres are served.

This is a win/win/win event. Your clients get a helpful golf lesson and useful investment information. The golf pro gets exposure to new customers for him and his club. You will have provided a fun venue to deepen your relationships and set the stage for a productive and well-received follow-up call to your clients.

What about the cost? As a successful advisor, you may cosponsor the clinic and tap into the resources available from sponsors, managers, or vendors with whom you do business. In the spirit of "we're all in this together," I have never worked with a firm that wasn't inclined to support advisors willing to use its products and services with clients.

Imagine this idea's potential. Are there other interests for which you can hold clinics? For me, tennis comes to mind.

## #6 TAKE ME OUT TO THE BALLGAME

Baseball is a spring ritual and has been a tremendous relationship builder for fathers and sons for years. A few years back, I took my son to spring training in Florida. We traveled from town to town visiting the various parks and watching some great baseball. Not only did we watch terrific baseball, but we also created some wonderful memories.

Why not take your clients and their kids out to the old ballpark for a game? Whether you sponsor a trip to a major league game, a minor league game, or a college game really doesn't matter. The memories you create will not soon be forgotten.

The advisors I've worked with who have used this idea make it a regular, anticipated springtime event. Whether it's a father taking his son or a grandfather taking his grandson, everyone has a fun time. Sure, organizing an event like this takes a little time and effort, but it is something that every advisor can do. So play ball.

## #7 PICTURES FROM A FRIEND

I had one advisor who would always make the most of all his travel—personal and business. Prior to going to a conference or taking a trip, he would prepare a postcard mailing to his clients to be sent from the conference city.

He'd literally box up the cards and take them with him on the plane and to the hotel. He wanted to get the postmark from the city where the conference was being held. By sending a personal postcard from the conference city to his clients, thanking them for their business, he further increased his credibility with them.

Clients want to be regularly reminded that they are important to you. This advisor used this creative postcard idea to stay top of mind with his clients and demonstrate that he not only remembered them but was at this meeting to get additional training to continue to deliver world-class service to them.

**Clients want to be regularly reminded that they are important to you.**

**It's not up to your clients to remember you. It's your job to constantly remind them of who you are and reinforce why they have a relationship with you.**

What pictures or events can you use in your next Gratitude Marketing™ mailing? Clients love to receive fun and humorous mail. It's another point of connection. When you think about it, *it's not up to your clients to remember you. It's your job to constantly remind them of who you are and reinforce why they have a relationship with you.*

 THE LAGNIAPPE—BIG SHOES TO FILL

Early in my career, I identified a firm that I really wanted to be part of. I contacted the management and flew up to their home office and interviewed. But to my disappointment, I didn't receive a response. I decided it was time for a little creativity.

I went to the store and bought a brand-new pair of black dress shoes. I enclosed a note with the shoes and sent them to my prospective employer. The note read, "I look forward to wearing out the leather on these soles to help your firm reach its goals."

What happened? I got a call from the firm the next day, and I went on to enjoy a very successful career with that company. How can you adapt an idea like this to work for you? Is there a prospect you need to connect with in a unique way?

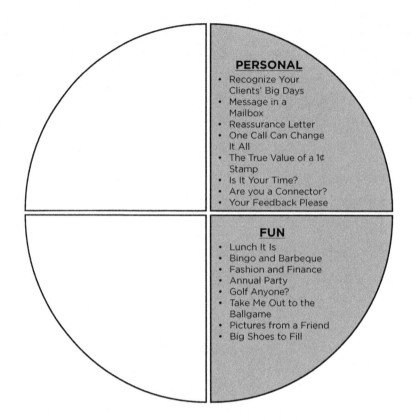

## MAKING IT FUN RECAP

Can you see how adding a little fun can enhance your practice? What I've found is that if you are bit creative and even, sometimes, different in your approach, your efforts will be greatly appreciated and your clients will always recognize your creativity. You can make Gratitude Marketing™ your humble assistant and your companion on the road to significance. Using your creativity and injecting a little fun into your relationships will be a key factor that will make you a trusted presence in your clients' eyes and keep them with you for life.

# CHAPTER 6

# Making it Seasonal

*I follow three rules: do the right thing, do the best you can, and always show people you care.*

—Lou Holtz

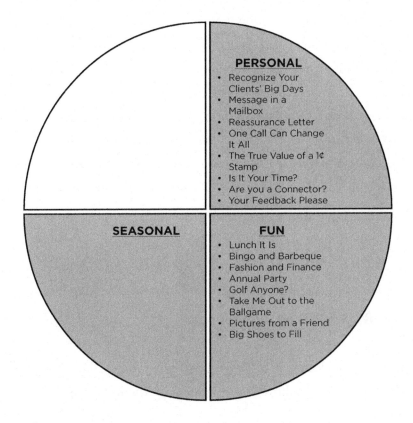

**PERSONAL**
- Recognize Your Clients' Big Days
- Message in a Mailbox
- Reassurance Letter
- One Call Can Change It All
- The True Value of a 1¢ Stamp
- Is It Your Time?
- Are you a Connector?
- Your Feedback Please

**SEASONAL**

**FUN**
- Lunch It Is
- Bingo and Barbeque
- Fashion and Finance
- Annual Party
- Golf Anyone?
- Take Me Out to the Ballgame
- Pictures from a Friend
- Big Shoes to Fill

The holidays offer another tremendous opportunity to make a memorable connection. They are a magical time of year for celebration and fellowship. Make the holidays happy for your clients and their families, and they will make you happy all year long.

Every holiday season, our family plans a time together to watch *It's a Wonderful Life*. As James Stewart demonstrated in his role in the film, participating in and influencing many people's lives matters tremendously. The movie, directed by Frank Capra, premiered on December 20, 1946, at New York's Globe Theater. George Bailey, the main character, played by Stewart, ended up staying in his hometown of Bedford Falls and taking over his father's business, the Bailey Building and Loan.

What most people don't realize is the inspiration for the film came from Philip Van Doren Stern, who had originally titled the story, *The Greatest Gift*. George Bailey did, indeed, have a gift—for helping people. Van Doren Stern's view is shared by many:

> *I rejoice in life for its own sake. Life is no "brief candle" to me. It is a sort of splendid torch which I have got hold of for the moment, and I want to make it burn as brightly as possible before handing it on to future generations.*
>
> —GEORGE BERNARD SHAW

> *It is one of the most beautiful compensations in life that no man can sincerely try to help another without helping himself.*
>
> —RALPH WALDO EMERSON

Let's take a close look at seven gifts/lessons from *It's A Wonderful Life* and consider how you might apply them to your life and business.

1. One of the key lessons George's dad relayed to him was that the choices you make today really are important. Are you here to make a living or to make a difference in the lives of your clients?

2. Your future is determined by what you believe and do. Every one of your beliefs generates behavior, and every behavior has a consequence. Thus, you become what you believe and do every day.

**Are you here to make a living or to make a difference in the lives of your clients?**

3. You're closer to your breakthrough than you think. You're where you are at this moment in time for a reason. Although George Bailey toyed with the idea of seeking his fame and fortune elsewhere, his life mattered to too many in Bedford Falls.

4. Wisdom isn't just what you know but also how you live. George's dad demonstrated this to him and his brother daily by his actions.

5. The greatest use of life is to spend it for something that will outlast it.

6. Encourage others to talk about themselves by asking questions. Over the years, because George was there for his clients in good and bad times, he cultivated a multitude of trust.

7. Sometimes, you have to step back and look at things from a new perspective before you move forward. This will give you a greater appreciation for what you already have. George Bailey had a passion for helping people. He understood that success is often fleeting, but the impact of helping people lasts a lifetime and beyond.

**So how can you create memories for your client?**

So how can you create memories for your client? Let me share ideas that you can use in your Gratitude Marketing™ to make it seasonal.

## HOLIDAY SEASON NIGHT AT THE THEATER

Host a holiday season night at the theater. Send a letter out to your clients, inviting them to a special holiday show at the theater. Limit the number of free tickets and make it first-come, first-served. Then rent a bus. Have your clients meet and park at your office to ride together to the theater on the bus. Your clients will enjoy a wonderful evening of live theater, memories will be created, and you can make it a regular event in your practice. A side benefit of this event will be the positive word-of-mouth attention to your practice in the community.

FIGURE 6.1

 RENT A MOVIE THEATER

Not much goes on at your local movie theater on Saturday mornings, so why not approach the manager with this idea: Since the theater has a fixed cost during this time period but no revenue, ask if the management would consider letting you rent the theater on a Saturday morning to invite your clients for a special showing of a holiday classic. You should be able to negotiate a reasonable rental rate and a discounted rate for the refreshments.

Invite your clients and their families, children, and/or grandchildren to take time out together from the hustle and bustle of the season and get in the spirit. Before the movie, give each child a small soft drink and a bag of popcorn. If you want, you can even hire a Santa Claus to come and take a photograph with all the children. This will save your clients the hassle of taking their kids to the mall to have pictures taken and provide them with a lifelong memory. If you really want to take this idea to the next level, get specialty photo frames made up and have the photo of the child with Santa placed in a frame that comes from your firm. Put your name on the back, not the front, of the frame. That way, each year when your clients take the photo out, they'll be reminded of where they got it. Little things like that have unbelievable top-of-mind staying power from year to year.

*Feeling gratitude and not expressing it is like wrapping a present and not giving it.*

—WILLIAM ARTHUR WARD

## UNEXPECTED GIFTS

When you think of the holidays, gifts are a big part of the season. We've all heard that it's not the gift but the thought that matters. The truth is you can't underestimate the impact of a well-timed gift. If you're going to budget for gifts to your clients, why not make them practical? You can offer gratitude 24/7 by sending top-of-mind gift items that are retained and used over and over again. They can deliver the level of measurement you expect in your marketing effort.

Before we go on, consider this: 74 percent of American consumers surveyed reported having at least one promotional product in their workspace; 83 percent reported they liked receiving promotional products with an advertising message; and 89 percent of consumers could recall the name of the advertiser on a promotional product they had received in the past 24 months. How's that for top-of-mind impact?

Years ago we lived in a new subdivision that was being built out. We were one of the first 50 houses in the subdivision that, once completed, included 800+ homes. One real estate agent wanted to be the agent for the subdivision. She decided to deliver to all the residents' mailboxes, every month, a promotional item with her name prominently displayed on it. In her case, she chose to deliver kitchen items, such as jar grips, measuring cups and spoons, and so on. We used to joke in the neighborhood that we all had kitchens by Judy. Did this strategy work for Judy? Did it ever! In her second year in the business, she not only sold our home but also about 30 others in the subdivision. She had laid claim to our subdivision and cultivated top-of-mind awareness among our residents through promotional marketing.

Because of your ability to target to a specific group, your cost is lower per lasting impression than most other forms of marketing. There are professionals who can help you focus specifically on designing and implementing customer gift programs. Over the past 25 years, I've worked with one of the industry's best: Park Printing. This company has consistently provided me with creative ideas to execute this aspect of Gratitude Marketing™.

I asked Park Muhlheizler of Park Printing to illustrate how he stood out in his business and how he has continually helped companies realize that, while other companies were spending marketing dollars on other forms of media, his form of marketing puts ideas into the hands of the people actually doing the buying: your clients.

Park listed four key guideposts:

**Guidepost 1:** Calculate your activity levels. Park started Park Printing from nothing. His first days in the promotional business were tough, as he had never made a sales call and had no idea of even the basic terminology of the promotional industry. But what he did have was a real drive to make this new opportunity work, a sense of what buyers needed, and, of course, a monthly mortgage as a pragmatic motivator. He figured if he made ten cold calls each day, for roughly 250 business days in a year, he would total 2,500 contacts in a calendar year. He calculated that if he were lucky and good enough to hit 5 percent, he would get more business than he could handle. What actually happened is that, after four months, he never had to make another cold call for the rest of his career.

**Guidepost 2:** Enjoy your days. Every company uses some type of promotional product. Park decided to prospect for individuals at companies that made it enjoyable for him to go work each day and that appreciated the importance of developing a working relationship with him. He was able to convince buyers that since he had spent years on their side of the desk, they could trust him to get things going for them. The feeling that people trusted him with their business was immediate confirmation that they saw the value in what he had to provide. That expression of faith was uplifting beyond belief.

**Guidepost 3:** Admit that you're not all-knowing. The early days of prospecting were opportunities to learn more, so Park paid attention to what his soon-to-be new clients told him about how other providers had fallen down and what he needed to do to make their days easier. He took the time to learn from what they were telling him. He took what they taught him and become more knowledgeable. By doing so, he was able to give them what they actually wanted.

**Expressing gratitude consistently is a way of life. It's a conscious effort to show your appreciation.**

**Guidepost 4:** Bring people along on the journey and make it personal. Park let his clients know how important they were to him. He also kept them in the loop as to how he was doing. There's no better way to start each day than to have others cheerleading for you. Park would cheerlead for them as well. It's an amazing truism that givers get.

Expressing gratitude consistently is a way of life. It's a conscious effort to show your appreciation. How expensive is it to use top-of-mind promotional gifts? Let's assume that you have a 12-month budget of $1,000 a month and you have 200–350 perspective clients you want to approach. A proven monthly program would look like this:

**January:** Post-it notes, $1 to $2 each.

**February**: Candy jars, $3 to $4 each.

**March:** Chip clips, $1 to $2 each.

**April:** Baseball cards, $1.50 to $2.50 each.

**May:** Sport bottles, $2 to $5 dollars each.

**June:** Divot repair tools, $0.50 to $5 each.

**July**: Jar openers, $0.75 to $1.50 each.

**August:** Fortune cookies, $0.40 to $0.60 each.

**September:** Stress balls, $1 to $3 each.

**October:** Piggy banks, $2 to $4 each.

**November:** Calendars or mouse pads, $1 or $5 each.

**December:** Christmas gifts, Christmas cards, $1.75 to $2 each.

*(Keep in mind the individual items can be changed depending on your preferences.)*

Then you can put together a proven seasonal program for a more wide-ranging budget. In the spring, you can send items such as seed packets for flowers, candy, race T-shirts, or Frisbees. In the summer, consider mailing stadium cups, beach balls, grilling accessories, beach towels, sunglasses, sunscreen, or golf shirts. For the fall, try football seat cushions, umbrellas, throw blankets, or hand sanitizers. And for winter, send your clients lip balm, hand lotion, Thanksgiving cards, holiday cards, and chocolates. It would be wise not to assume that your clients remember all the services you offer. Having this kind of regular plan to stay in touch and remind them of all your services provides lasting top-of-mind value. If you would like to work with Park, he may be reached at (502) 241-6036 or via e-mail at parkprintingky@gmail.com. You may also visit his website at www.parkprintingky.com

My point is that when you find people you trust, who know their business the way Park does, you can basically give them a budget and leave it in their hands to put together something that works. All of us want a vendor we like and trust and who has been down the path.

 **FACE OF THE HOLIDAYS**

Successful financial advisors understand the importance of this five-step connection process: (1) you establish the relationship, (2) you nurture the relationship, (3) you transact business, (4) you service accounts, and (5) you keep on doing it, and it becomes a circular process.

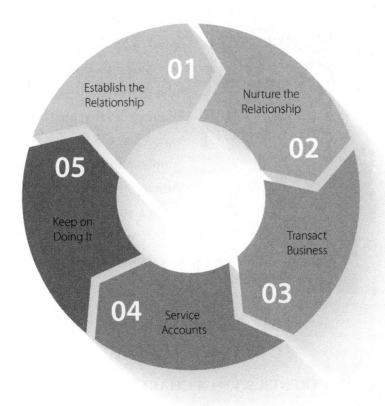

FIGURE 6.2

Would you like a way to show up and stand out during each holiday during the year? Send your clients a picture postcard of yourself in a holiday setting.

This idea doesn't have to be limited to Christmas. You can send a postcard on any holiday: Thanksgiving, Fourth of July, Easter, or Halloween. I'm not talking about going up to Manhattan and taking a picture by the toy soldier in front of FAO Schwarz. I'm talking about very down-to-earth pictures, such as a photo of you and your wife in a pumpkin patch or, maybe, on July 4, a photo of you and your family at the beach. It's all about the thought. It's all about including you. It's humanizing you, making your clients feel that you're just another person. A recent global investment

FIGURE 6.3

survey found that investors spend 475 hours or more per year worrying about money. That's one hour and 20 minutes a day, nine hours a week, or 475 hours a year. Simply put: the more you show up, the more you can remind your clients not to worry and reassure them that they are in your capable hands.

 **PARTNER WITH A CHARITY**

I work with a couple of advisors who really capture the spirit of the holidays. Every year, they host a holiday party for their clients. When they send out the invitation, they ask their clients to bring a toy to the party that will be donated to a charitable organization that provides needy children with a special Christmas. It's a wonderful example of a lot of people who are each doing a little but making a big difference in the lives of these children. Would some variation of this work for you? You never know how what you're doing with an idea like this might affect others. As Winston Churchill observed, "We make a living by what we get, but we make a life by what we give."

## MAKE A DONATION

In recent years, I've seen a number of advisors send their clients holiday cards wishing them not only greetings of the season but also stating that, on their behalf, a donation has been made to a particular charity. This is a heartwarming way to express gratitude in addition to, or in lieu of, a gift. Is there a need within your own community that's appropriate for this idea? Gratitude Marketing™ involves a diversity of gestures and experiences that are only limited by the degree of your creativity and implementation. As Barbara Bush said, "Giving frees us from the familiar territory of our own needs by opening our mind to the unexplained worlds occupied by the needs of others."

## HOST AN ANNUAL NEW YEAR'S EVE PARTY

Now that the presents have all been exchanged between family and friends, let me ask what your plan is for New Years Eve. This is a very logical idea for you, as an advisor, to put to use at the time of the year when your area of expertise is top of mind.

Why? At the beginning of the year, clients are filled with renewed hope and generally make New Year's resolutions. Two of the top resolutions are to lose weight and to save money. Can you think of a better time to be face-to-face with your clients? As I begin each new year, I'm reminded of the words of management consultant Peter Drucker, who said, "The best way to predict the future is to create it."

Starting a new year is like being the first one on the ski lift on a beautiful sunny morning. There you are, at the top of the mountain, with your skis pointed down and ready to go through the fresh snow, ready to ski where no one has yet dared to go this morning. What makes this so exciting? It's the anticipation and the imagination of the run, *your* run. Your clients are experiencing the same feeling as they think about starting fresh on January 1.

Albert Einstein believed that "imagination is more important than knowledge, for knowledge is limited to all we now know and understand. While imagination embraces the entire world and all there would be to know and understand." The power and potential of embracing our possibilities and the magnitude of the opportunity in front of us, combined with a focus that the new year brings, gives us all a fresh dose of urgency.

And urgency is the driver for clients to make important decisions. Ask your clients three critical questions to help you make their new year extraordinary:

1. What personal sense of purpose is driving you in your personal and business life this year?

2. Whom do you plan to influence in a positive and lasting way this year?

3. What knowledge can you gain in the coming year that will benefit you?

Let me share a secret of many great achievers: they never consider themselves truly finished with their work. When the legendary Pablo Casals reached his 95th year, a reporter asked, "Mr. Casals, you're 95 and the greatest cellist who ever lived. Why do you still practice six hours a day?" Casals answered, "Because I think I'm making progress." We are all works in progress. Each new year brings with it the promise of a new beginning. We must continue to improve one day at a time.

 ## THE LAGNIAPPE—LARGER THAN LIFE

Want to get creative with your best clients? Go larger than life. Imagine the fun that you'll create when you deliver a four-foot by six-foot birthday card or a colorful bunch of balloons to your client's office. You pick the occasion or the season to really show up big. With Gratitude Marketing™, the point is to have fun and embrace the possibilities. And remember that "gratitude is a flower that blooms in noble souls," and I am quoting Pope Francis here.

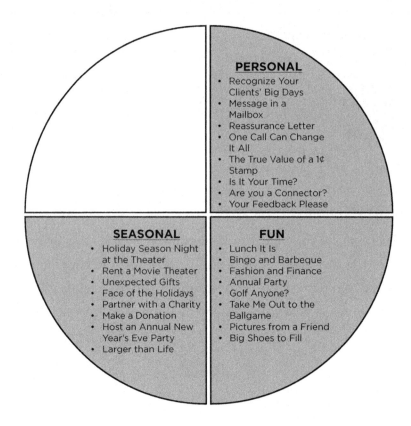

## MAKING IT SEASONAL RECAP

Think for a moment. What special events or activities can you start sponsoring on a regular annual or semiannual basis? Try it. If you allow your mind to think outside the box, you'll discover some terrific ideas that will stand out with your clients. Use Gratitude Marketing™ during the many seasons in the year as the foundation on which you build and nurture long-standing relationships.

# CHAPTER 7

# Making it Mindful

*As we express our gratitude, we must never forget that the highest appreciation is not to utter words, but to live by them.*

—JOHN F. KENNEDY

**MINDFUL**

**PERSONAL**
- Recognize Your Clients' Big Days
- Message in a Mailbox
- Reassurance Letter
- One Call Can Change It All
- The True Value of a 1¢ Stamp
- Is It Your Time?
- Are you a Connector?
- Your Feedback Please

**SEASONAL**
- Holiday Season Night at the Theater
- Rent a Movie Theater
- Unexpected Gifts
- Face of the Holidays
- Partner with a Charity
- Make a Donation
- Host an Annual New Year's Eve Party
- Larger than Life

**FUN**
- Lunch It Is
- Bingo and Barbeque
- Fashion and Finance
- Annual Party
- Golf Anyone?
- Take Me Out to the Ballgame
- Pictures from a Friend
- Big Shoes to Fill

In 2005, New Orleans was hit by the perfect storm. Life for many was changed forever. Through it all, Hurricane Katrina taught me a lot about the importance of gratitude. I saw businesses open their doors to people who weren't even their customers at the time just because these folks needed a helping hand. I saw more than one restaurant owner go out into the community and offer free food for the multitudes of volunteers who came to New Orleans to aid in the recovery. For these gestures of kindness, we will forever be grateful.

Whether or not these businesses realized it at the time, they were practicing Gratitude Marketing™. They were paying it forward and building lifelong relationships with people who were placed in their path by circumstance. At the time, I marveled at the ability to bring so much value to so many people without ever expecting anything in return. How have these businesses done in the ten years since the storm? In a word—magnificently.

The community has never forgotten their gracious gestures and remains fiercely loyal to these businesses. To me, these businesses are in the minds of their loyal clients because of the generosity they extended. Events occur all the time that give you the opportunity to master Gratitude Marketing™. By implementing a systematic plan, you can have an impact on more clients and inspire them to reach their financial goals. All you have to do is *make it mindful.*

*Do all the good you can, by all the means you can, and in all the ways you can, in all the places you can, and all the times you can, to all the people you can, as long as you ever can.*

—JOHN WESLEY

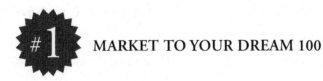

## MARKET TO YOUR DREAM 100

Most of the ideas presented in this book pertain to nurturing current client relationships. However, with the normal attrition inherent in our business, successful financial advisors also recognize the need to constantly cultivate relationships that will lead to new clients.

Put together a list of 100 prospects you feel would be ideal clients for you. These are the people you may convert to clients in six months or twelve months, or one, three, or five years. These are the people you believe are definitely worth the effort. Once the list is put together, ask yourself what you are going to do to market to your dream 100 each and every month without fail. Will you use:

1. Twitter?

2. Facebook?

3. LinkedIn?

4. Direct Mail?

5. Calls?

6. E-mail?

7. Promotional Items?

Your goal is to be *everywhere your clients and prospects are*, not just everywhere.

Successful gratitude marketers know they must first and constantly get their prospects' *attention* before they can get their *intention*. Once advisors realize their commitment and move forward, an increased level of certainty will continue to move them to action on a consistent basis.

**Successful gratitude marketers know they must first and constantly get their prospects' *attention* before they can get their *intention*.**

To help as many clients as possible discover the best way to live based on their financial means, ask yourself these four key questions and answer them by targeting your dream 100:

1. From your prospects' perspective, why should they do business with you?

2. What do you deliver that no one else can?

3. Why does your firm exist?

4. What distinguishes your firm from everyone else's?

Continuing to build and nurture your business requires a bit of time and a lot of relationships. You must be open and available to others around you.

Keep in mind that clients don't do anything until they are inspired. So frame your business to align with your clients' and prospects' needs. The time you spend now, going through this exercise, will pay big dividends later. As Abraham Lincoln advised, "Always bear in mind that your own resolution to succeed is more important than any one thing."

Go ahead and sharpen your focus on your dream 100. If *you* don't believe in your practice, no one else will. You have a great practice. Use Gratitude Marketing™ to tell the world about it.

## #2   WELCOME WAGON

Here's an idea I used when I started in the business many years ago. How many of you are familiar with Welcome Wagon? This company, which is more than 80 years old, is the world's largest welcoming service. One day, as I was cold-calling, I started thinking about the common denominator I needed to identify new clients. It was simple: change. But how could I locate prospects who were in the midst of change? All I had to do was pinpoint new people moving into town. Welcome Wagon was a game changer for me. This one idea enabled me to consistently open 30 to 35 new accounts a month.

How do you implement this idea? You contract with Welcome Wagon to be included in the mix when the Welcome Wagon representative goes to visit the new families moving into the area. During the visit, the Welcome Wagon representative provides the new family with a collection of items from the various businesses that have contracted with that organization. I provided the four-by-six card outlining my services that you see here.

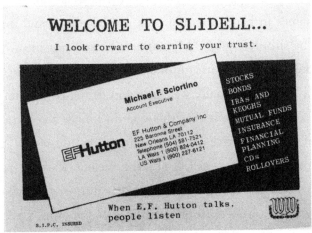

FIGURE 7.1

Then I got creative and wondered what item I could provide that would keep me top of mind with the recently relocated family. I reasoned that since they ate every day, they'd probably go to their refrigerator several times a day. Now, what is on just about every refrigerator? A picture of Little Johnny or Susie or their artwork from school posted front and center on the fridge door. What keeps those pictures up on the refrigerator? A magnet. So I created a magnet in the shape of a telephone. At the time, I worked for E.

FIGURE 7.2

F. Hutton, which had one of the best taglines ever for a firm in our business—"When E. F. Hutton talks…people listen."

Once the Welcome Wagon visits have been made, for a nominal fee per name, the Welcome Wagon representative sends business clients a list of all the families called on. With those names in hand, I would pick up the phone and introduce myself by simply saying, "My name is Mike Sciortino with E. F. Hutton. I am working in conjunction with Welcome Wagon, and I would like to personally welcome you to the community." The important point here is that this was no longer a cold call but a warm call to a receptive neighbor. Often, I would set up appointments on that very first call. If not, the Welcome Wagon recipient was placed on my mailing list for regular informative follow-ups. The leverage I gained from Welcome Wagon was a very cost-effective way of building my business, and it can do the same for yours. Today, Welcome Wagon uses the mail and Internet very effectively.

Top performers are top performers in our business because they are so determined to be top performers that they will do the things to be top performers that most advisors will never do. What's their secret? They take action now. They embrace ideas like this, and they execute them. After careful planning and through daily discipline, they realize that if it is to be, it is up to them to do it—now.

Why is getting it done *now* so important? Our clients and prospects have never needed us more. They are facing an increasing number of problems that they are unprepared to solve. They are fearful, frustrated, and beginning to doubt whether or not they have properly prepared for life's goals and challenges. They need your help *now*.

What you do *now* for them matters. Some people enter our lives and leave almost instantly. Others stay and forge such an impression on us that we're changed forever. Today you must be that person. Make an impact in a positive way *now*.

 ## PROMOTIONAL NAPKIN IDEA

"Life is really simple, but we insist on making it complicated," wrote Confucius. With all the noise in their lives, clients trust us to make their lives simple. Being too busy is most often used as an excuse for avoiding critically important but uncomfortable actions such as planning for retirement or saving for a child's college tuition.

Simple can be harder than complex to execute. You have to work hard to get your thinking clean and simple. But it's worth it in the end, because once you get there—once you simplify your story—your practice will flourish.

Let's look back to the good old days for a prime example of simplicity. Small-town doctors were masters at simply explaining a course of action for their patients. They knew all the technical jargon yet related to their patients in a very understandable manner.

Simplicity is the new sophistication. Complex communication breeds mistrust and inaction. Simplicity breeds deep understanding and action. Most of the language we use in our industry is scary and foreign to our clients. Tell them what you can do for them in simple language. Challenge yourself to constantly keep your language clear. In time, you'll acquire the skill to keep your message simple yet significant. In the words of Ronald Reagan, "They say the world has become too complex for simple answers. They are wrong. Keep it simple."

Here's an example of how one advisor borrowed a straightforward idea from another industry. The original business plan of Southwest Airlines had been drawn up on a napkin, and this advisor adapted it and applied it to his investment practice. Here's the Southwest napkin and the one he adapted.

**Complex communication breeds mistrust and inaction. Simplicity breeds deep understanding and action.**

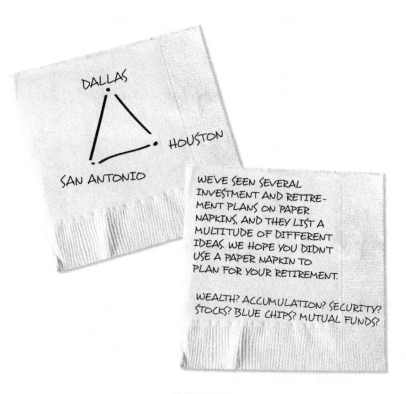

FIGURE 7.3

The original Southwest business plan was a triangle. At the top was Dallas, on the right was Houston, and on the bottom left was San Antonio. That was it. The business plan was that instead of people driving between those three cities, Southwest would simply fly them. The rest is history.

The advisor seized the concept. He took a napkin, and in the top left hand corner he wrote, "We've seen several investment and retirement plans on paper napkins, and they list a multitude of different ideas. We hope you didn't use a paper napkin to plan for your retirement."

He uses these napkins at all his events. You might provide your napkins to a local diner or restaurant. As you see, it's okay to appropriate ideas you see in other businesses and creatively adapt to your practice to stay ever mindful. In fact, it's what you should be doing every day.

*We talk about the quality of products and service.*
*What about the quality of our relationships and*
*the quality of our promises to each other?*

—MAX DEPREE

 ## SUBSCRIPTION ANYONE?

Before the days of instant news via the Internet, families depended on the morning and evening papers as their major sources of current information. For many, including me, the paper route became one of our first tastes for what it takes to run a business. But little did I know that I was also refining my Gratitude Marketing™ skills way back then.

What I learned was invaluable. The paper route taught me things such as dependability, responsibility, discipline, account-ability, and the social skills to interact with all types of people. But the most important lesson in marketing I learned from the experience was the power of staying top of mind on a regular basis with my clients.

Each year, the paper company would sponsor a trip for its paperboys. To win, we had to sell a certain number of new subscriptions. Back then Disney World in Florida had just opened. The contest rules stated that the paperboy who sold 25 new newspaper or magazine subscriptions would win a four-day trip to Disney World, all expenses paid. That was all the incentive I needed.

I tell this story to emphasize a few important points. Because I had serviced my existing clients so well, they gladly signed up for magazine subscriptions so I could win the trip. Here's the lesson: Because I had first given, I received. And if my clients weren't in a position to buy another subscription, they were happy to refer me to their neighbors.

What does this have to with our business? Over the years, many financial advisors I've worked with have successfully gifted subscriptions to their clients for various publications. In addition to business publications, you can gift subscriptions to magazines that may appeal to your clients' hobbies and interests. This gives you an opportunity to stay top of mind with your clients every single month in a very cost-effective way with very little continuous effort. It's just one more way for you to connect and cultivate that long-term relationship.

 **SPONSORSHIPS**

Sponsorships represent a true win/win. The school or organization wins through your generosity, and you win from the excellent exposure for your business. Here are two examples I've seen advisors use that stood out in terms of creativity and top-of-mind staying power:

1. Sponsor an essay contest. If you want to stir the creative juices of youth in your community to focus on solutions for their own future, contact a school in your community and propose an essay contest. Consult with

the faculty to agree on a mindful and appropriate topic, such as self-development.

This is just one example of the kind of topic that will inspire our youth. The prize you offer could be a gift card, small scholarship, or another prize determined by the faculty. As a sponsor, you are showing gratitude by giving back to your own community and paying it forward. This can easily turn into a regular event underwritten by your business. This is an idea to get you known in the community as the guy who does good things for people. It establishes you as the guy who gives back to the community. This is an easy idea to implement *now*.

2. One advisor I know very well created a different kind of sponsorship. In most places, high school football is big, really big. Friday nights are when members of the community gather, connect, and pull for their favorite team. These games present many opportunities for you to stand up and stand out by utilizing the sponsorships that are readily available. Every year, this advisor sponsors his local high school football team. His sponsorship includes a banner displayed on the fence around the field and the PA announcer's focus on his firm at the home game he sponsors.

As a sponsor, he's required to supply a promotional item for the fans at the game he sponsors. His business is in the Deep South, where many weeks during football season are really hot. He wisely chose, as his premium item, a handheld fan with the team roster on one side and his contact information on the other. He provides the fan at an early game each year, and people bring them to the next five or six games. It is a phenomenal idea because it's got staying power to keep his business top of mind in the community.

## #6 SHAREHOLDER MEETINGS

Aren't your clients who own mutual funds or stocks shareholders? Why not hold an annual shareholders meeting to offer them timely updates? One of my top producers executed this strategy brilliantly. Every year, he and I would gather his clients together over dinner to provide information on the current markets. We would do that by weaving in stories, not just focusing on facts. One of my earliest mentors shared this idea with me. He said, "Never forget facts tell, but stories sell." What we did was take the performance facts and intertwine them with stories instead of just getting up there and saying, "With this strategy, performance was up by X percent." You know what that statement means to clients? It means nothing. You need to tell them what it means. You need to merge those raw facts into a story about what they mean to your clients. Facts satisfy the analytical part of our brain, but it is stories that touch our hearts.

**Stories are the way we explain things. Stories are the gifts that we share. Stories are like pieces in a puzzle: they connect you to your clients.**

Storytelling is one of the oldest, most effective forms of

communication. Stories are the way we explain things. Stories are the gifts that we share. Stories are like pieces in a puzzle: they connect you to your clients. As John Steinbeck put it, "If a story is not about the hearer, he [or she] will not listen." Clients remember stories.

From the time we were kids, stories have captured our imagination. Remember hearing "Let me tell you a story"? Whether it was from a family member (grandparents are famous for this), a coach, a teacher, or even an actor in a movie, it is through stories that we have learned so many valuable lessons. Why should your business be any different? Sure, facts and numbers are vital to what we do, but your clients understand them better if the information is communicated in a way they can relate to. Sometimes, ideas need to be felt and heard. Through stories, your clients can envision change.

Stories work particularly well when you can illustrate your point in a way that highlights what's in it for your clients. This advisor knew that his clients would be more inclined to implement his recommendations if he connected to them by using a story that was easy to understand, easy to follow, and hard to forget.

When you examine the research on how storytelling affects the brain, you'll find that a story activates a part of the brain that allows listeners to turn the story into their own ideas and experience thanks to a process called neural coupling. People learn and retain information best when they are told it in an interesting story. Stories convert the facts we encounter in life into more meaningful experiences.

**Stories convert the facts we encounter in life into more meaningful experiences.**

The best stories you will ever tell are the ones your clients can retell to their friends and family, which will usually lead to unsolicited referrals for you. Great stories compel your clients to change the way they feel, the way they think, and even the way they behave. The stories that have engaged your clients for years work just as well today. That's the one thing that has not changed. After all, who doesn't like a good story?

 ## QUARTERLY CLIENT REVIEWS

Every day, you have the opportunity to do something wonderful for your clients. Most successful advisors I know are always trying to find that extraordinary breakthrough that allows them to serve their clients better. Sometimes that breakthrough is simply the broad perspective and experience they offer to their clients as they guide them to reach prudent decisions.

In any set of circumstances your clients may face, their own perspective will determine their response unless you are there to guide them. Therefore, it is vital that you allow them to share with you their core concerns, needs, and feelings at your client meetings. I would strongly suggest meeting with your clients at least quarterly to stay focused on their needs and address any changes that may have occurred. In most cases, these reviews uncover additional areas in which you can do business with your clients. Here are some thoughts to consider as you prepare for the meeting:

- What have they liked most and least about past investments they have made?

- What problems do they have that you can help them solve?

- What needs do they currently have?

- What solutions can you offer?

- What are their hopes and fears and how have they changed?

- What questions do they have?

- What do they already think or know about what you'll discuss?

- Who is the driving force behind the decision?

- What outcome would they like to see?

- How easy will it be for them to stick to the plan that you put together for them?

My experience as a retail advisor, in addition to my career as a wholesaler and head of distribution working with financial advisors and their clients, has made me appreciate that the time spent getting answers to these questions will build trust and solidify the relationship with your client. It will allow you to provide a higher level of service that focuses on their needs, wants, and goals. As an advisor, you are in a unique position to influence your clients and give them important reasons to change a habit—the way they save, for example—that will make a huge difference in their lives. Once they have explained their situation to their advisor, most clients just want their advisor to tell them what to do. It's usually as simple as that.

## #8   THE LAGNIAPPE—IN THE NEWS

In our business, consistency counts. It's what separates the enduringly successful advisors from the others. I'll never forget one advisor in particular, and to this day, I admire him for his consistency. This advisor was then in his mid-50s, and what impresses me most is that he is still using a marketing idea he used when he started in the business 30 years ago, because it still works.

Every week, he takes the local newspaper and cuts out pictures of people who have been promoted. He then sends them a card with that picture enclosed. On the front, the card reads, "You're in the news." On the inside, it reads, "We at [firm name] want to be the first to wish you the best of luck." When he calls to follow up, his chances of reaching that person are much better than if he were making a cold call because he stood up and recognized their accomplishments, something that other advisors had failed to do.

## BONUS   BONUS LAGNIAPPE—RICHES IN NICHES

The thirty-third idea in this edition of Gratitude Marketing™ is called riches in niches.

Just a few weeks ago, I helped one of the top advisors in one of our client firms host an evening event. The advisor had rented out a restaurant. I arrived to find 12 tables set up for 12 sponsors of investment products to distribute materials to the advisor's clients as they arrived. Here's how the evening unfolded. From 6:00 to 7:00 p.m., the advisor's clients circulated and visited with the representative from each of the investment firms. As their visit with each firm was completed, clients were given a raffle ticket to be used later that evening. At 7:00 p.m., everyone sat down at individual round tables for dinner with a representative from each of the sponsor firms. This setup encouraged and stimulated ongoing discussions between the representative of the firm and the advisor's clients in a relaxed, social setting.

At about 7:10 p.m., the advisor got up and addressed his clients. Now, here is where the niche plays a role, as all his clients were Asian, and he addressed them in their native language. The advisor first introduced all the representatives of the sponsor firms, and then, every 15 minutes after that, he stood back up to focus on one of the investment firms, give a brief update, and draw three to five names for the raffle. This went on for three hours. An added twist was that the representatives of the sponsor firms rotated tables about every hour, thus allowing them the opportunity to visit with more than one table of clients.

This advisor used a very relaxed environment to express gratitude to his clients as well as to very deliberately inform them of the various opportunities he could offer them on a one-on-one basis. He did not stop selling for three hours. It was one of the most engaging events I have ever experienced in my life. The fact that he was able to talk to this group of clients in Chinese illustrates the importance of communicating your message in a direct fashion.

**MINDFUL**
- Market to Your Dream 100
- Welcome Wagon
- Promotional Napkin Idea
- Subscription Anyone?
- Sponsorships
- Shareholder Meetings
- Quarterly Client Reviews
- In the News
- Riches in Niches

**PERSONAL**
- Recognize Your Clients' Big Days
- Message in a Mailbox
- Reassurance Letter
- One Call Can Change It All
- The True Value of a 1¢ Stamp
- Is It Your Time?
- Are you a Connector?
- Your Feedback Please

**SEASONAL**
- Holiday Season Night at the Theater
- Rent a Movie Theater
- Unexpected Gifts
- Face of the Holidays
- Partner with a Charity
- Make a Donation
- Host an Annual New Year's Eve Party
- Larger than Life

**FUN**
- Lunch It Is
- Bingo and Barbeque
- Fashion and Finance
- Annual Party
- Golf Anyone?
- Take Me Out to the Ballgame
- Pictures from a Friend
- Big Shoes to Fill

## MAKING IT MINDFUL RECAP

As I have repeatedly indicated throughout this book, if you don't consistently stay in touch with your clients, they may leave you from lack of communication.

Are you tired of being the best-kept secret in your community? As you've seen, Gratitude Marketing™ allows some flexibility in how you use it and offers you proven ideas. Which ideas can you start implementing in the next 30 days?

# CHAPTER 8

# Making Gratitude Marketing™ Work for You

*Human beings, by changing the inner attitudes of their minds, can change the outer aspects of their lives.*

—WILLIAM JAMES

When I sat down to write this book, I started with one basic question: What ideas would I love to have if I were beginning again? I've cherry-picked for you the best of the proven ideas that have worked for other successful financial advisors. Now my job is to help you easily execute them step by step.

The main thing that separates successful advisors from average producers is the ability to be open to, and learn from, new information and then implement what they've learned.

**The main thing that separates successful advisors from average producers is the ability to be open to, and learn from, new information and then implement what they've learned.**

We all learn from experience—ours and the experience of others. To paraphrase Mark Twain, a wise man learns from his own mistakes, but a genius learns from others. Gratitude Marketing™ will solidify your relationships with your clients but only if you use it consistently. It cannot be a one-off strategy for your business. That's why I've included the system tools to assist you in applying incremental ideas on a regular basis. Once the system is established, you will see how it can easily be repeated.

Gratitude Marketing™ requires you to use CARE, which stands for

**C** — consistent

**A** — appreciation

**R** — regularly

**E** — everyday

Why do all these ideas work so well? Because your clients appreciate your recognition. Ralph Waldo Emerson wrote, "You cannot do a kindness too soon, but you never know how soon it will be too late." My goal is to help you make Gratitude Marketing™ a game changer for your practice.

*If we did all the things in life we are capable of doing, we would literally astound ourselves.*

**—THOMAS EDISON**

Is it luck or talent that makes successful financial advisors experience what others wish for but never attain? Happily, success has little to do with extraordinary luck or talent. Instead, successful financial advisors share two unique qualities. You don't have to be innately gifted with these qualities. Each of them can be acquired, learned, and developed. The two qualities are (1) having a dream and (2) staying focused on it. The ability to stay focused is not a gift or a talent. It is a decision. Successful advisors say yes to their dreams and no to distractions. They develop a plan and implement it. You can too.

Before we begin the implementation steps, I'd like to ask you to do three important things. All three are game changers.

1. Start using a Gratitude Marketing™ business creation journal today. At the top of each page write, "Today I will [list one major activity]." This will tie in nicely to your timetable for action and your commitment log that I will share with you in a second. You take one step a day, and you will be 365 times better at the end of the year.

2. Write down the three main things that executing your Gratitude Marketing™ plan will enable you to do, to be, to have, or to enjoy. This will help you acknowledge your commitment to this plan and drive you to implement it. "The will to win, the desire to succeed, the urge to reach your full potential, these are the keys that will unlock the door to personal excellence" (Confucius). The word is *commitment*. I have found that commitment is the shared trait among successful advisors. Make no mistake about it. Behind all great successes, there's a will—that is usually followed by hard work.

3. Focus your Fridays. I know many successful financial advisors who set aside one Friday a month to get *out of the* business and work purely *on the* business not *in the* business. This exercise in clarity allows them to step

aside, look at the big picture, reflect, relax, and refocus. Consider these four questions:

- What did I learn about my practice in the last 30 days?

- How can I use this to improve or enhance my life or my business?

- Using what I've learned, what can I do better?

- What do I want my business to look like five years from now?

How are you going to find the time to do this? Like a turtle, you can only make progress if you are willing to stick your neck out and embrace the possibilities. Why are these Focus Fridays critical? Well, as Jim Rohn pointed out, "If you don't design your own life plan, chances are you'll fall into someone else's plan. And guess what they might plan for you? Not much." Unless you're focused on the passions of your heart and are striving toward them, you won't achieve all that's in store for you.

*To become what we are capable of becoming is the only end in life.*

—ROBERT LOUIS STEVENSON

Gratitude Marketing™ is a proven, sustainable system to get you where you want to go. Once you realize what you're capable of, the whole world changes. The legendary UCLA coach John Wooden used to say, "Don't measure yourself by what you have accomplished but by what you have accomplished with your ability." Coach Wooden was a master at helping players realize their true potential. He believed when you learn something you must be quick to implement what you learned. Applying many of his lessons, several of his players achieved success beyond their wildest dreams both on the court and in life.

When I look at the lives of extraordinary financial advisors, I find that most were able to say *no to the unimportant* so that they could say *yes to the important*, whatever that was in their lives. They passionately believed that wherever they were in life, they could do better. I also found that the earlier in life they began playing to their strengths, as opposed to their weaknesses, the more opportunities they developed and enjoyed.

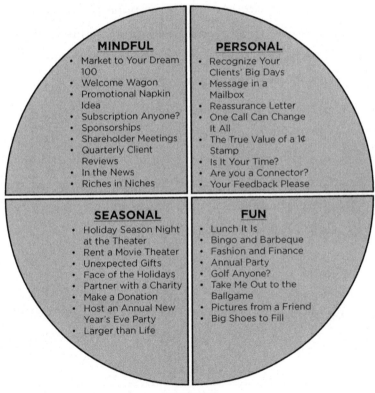

**MINDFUL**
- Market to Your Dream 100
- Welcome Wagon
- Promotional Napkin Idea
- Subscription Anyone?
- Sponsorships
- Shareholder Meetings
- Quarterly Client Reviews
- In the News
- Riches in Niches

**PERSONAL**
- Recognize Your Clients' Big Days
- Message in a Mailbox
- Reassurance Letter
- One Call Can Change It All
- The True Value of a 1¢ Stamp
- Is It Your Time?
- Are you a Connector?
- Your Feedback Please

**SEASONAL**
- Holiday Season Night at the Theater
- Rent a Movie Theater
- Unexpected Gifts
- Face of the Holidays
- Partner with a Charity
- Make a Donation
- Host an Annual New Year's Eve Party
- Larger than Life

**FUN**
- Lunch It Is
- Bingo and Barbeque
- Fashion and Finance
- Annual Party
- Golf Anyone?
- Take Me Out to the Ballgame
- Pictures from a Friend
- Big Shoes to Fill

FIGURE 8.1

Let's walk through the seven steps for putting into practice your Gratitude Marketing™ system. With platforms such as Salesforce and Google calendars, you can sync your calendar with others on your staff to easily coordinate your efforts.

**Step 1:** Select a Gratitude Marketing™ idea from each of the four categories we covered in the last four chapters. For example, in the Personal category, you might select the idea of handwritten notes or letters. In the Fun category, you might choose the idea of a birthday lunch. In the Seasonal category, you might decide on the idea of a holiday season night at the theater. And in the Mindful category, you might really like the Welcome Wagon idea. Ideas are the most powerful force in the marketplace, and once you've prioritized a few, you will find that *what* you prioritized will shape your future. By using Gratitude Marketing™, you are learning not to just sell but, more importantly, to be interested in your client as a person.

**Step 2:** What would it take for you to implement each of these ideas? How will you involve your staff? From experience, I can assure you that your ability to focus is one of the most important keys to the success of your Gratitude Marketing™ program. It's the master skill for achieving your goals and realizing your dreams.

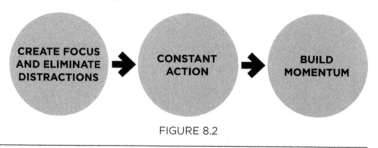

FIGURE 8.2

The Gratitude Marketing™ tools featured in figures 8.3–8.8 are available for download in PDF format at:

**GratitudeMarketingBook.com**

**Step 3:** Use the "My Commitments" template.

---

# MY COMMITMENTS

In each of the next 6 months, if I:

Month 1: _____

Month 2: _____

Month 3: _____

Month 4: _____

Month 5: _____

Month 6: _____

Then...

1. _____

2. _____

3. _____

4. _____

5. _____

6. _____

No matter what—Do at least one thing each day to create new business.

### Remember:
**"We are what we repeatedly do.
Excellence then, is not an act, but a habit."
– Aristotle**

---

FIGURE 8.3

Write down your commitments. Peter Drucker stresses, "Unless commitment is made, there are only promises and hopes but no plans." Today is where tomorrow's success lies. An example of that kind of commitment is our Olympic athletes. Study the sacrifices and choices they make in order to achieve their dreams. Look at the obstacles they overcome, the commitments they pledge to their sport, their perseverance, their relentless and contagious spirit, and most of all, the way they nurture their mind-set. They achieve because they believe they can, and as Abraham Lincoln said, "Let no feelings of discouragement prey upon you, and in the end you are sure to succeed."

These athletes succeed because they enthusiastically embrace the possibilities, just as you are doing with Gratitude Marketing™. They realize that due to their hard work, day in and day out, a new possibility can spin off in an entirely new direction. They are awake to the present moment and all it has to offer. They consistently fill their minds with the healthiest and most powerful and vital thoughts. They understand the importance of attitude.

*Nothing can stop the man with the right mental attitude from achieving his goals; nothing on earth can help the man with the wrong mental attitude.*

**—THOMAS JEFFERSON**

Olympic athletes never discount the difference attitude makes. This, combined with their relentless focus on the little things, makes them the world-class athletes they are. The same approach can work for you in your practice to make you a world-class marketer.

**Step 4:** Get your activities placed on the Gratitude Marketing™ calendar.

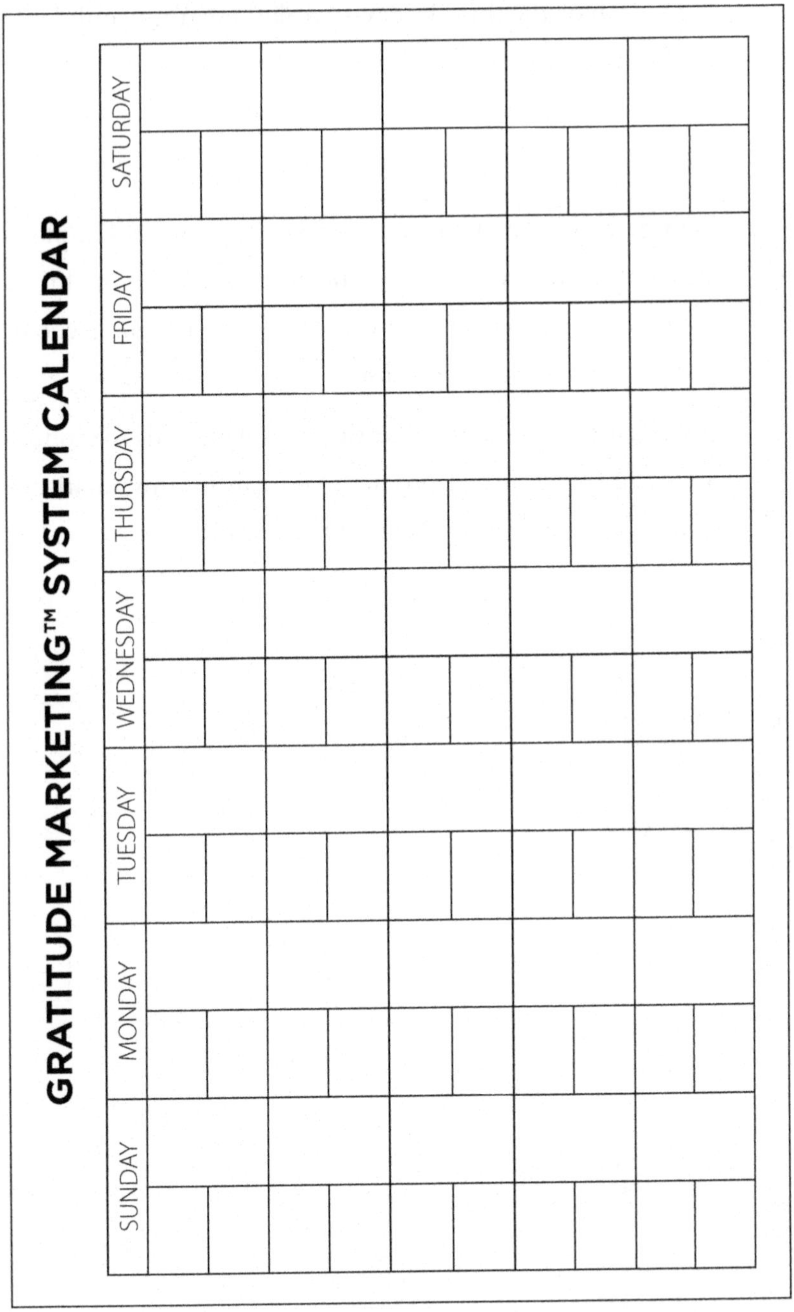

FIGURE 8.4

This includes scheduling your Focus Fridays. I find using the same Friday each month—for example, the first Friday of the month or the third Friday—works best. Your confidence in this system grows by doing, not just by thinking. Only actions—deliberate, well-coordinated actions—produce results.

**Step 5**: Utilize the Gratitude Marketing™ system templates to chart your progress. I've included a thank-you log, a mailing log, a promotion or campaign planner, and a client-gathering planner for your use.

Just as a master craftsman uses the tools of his trade to produce a magnificent finished product, you can use my Gratitude Marketing™ tools to mold and refine your business.

# THANK YOU LOG

| | Name | Date | Topic Discussed | Phone, Mail, or Email | Follow-up Needed |
|---|---|---|---|---|---|
| 1 | | | | | |
| 2 | | | | | |
| 3 | | | | | |
| 4 | | | | | |
| 5 | | | | | |
| 6 | | | | | |
| 7 | | | | | |
| 8 | | | | | |
| 9 | | | | | |
| 10 | | | | | |
| 11 | | | | | |
| 12 | | | | | |
| 13 | | | | | |
| 14 | | | | | |
| 15 | | | | | |
| 16 | | | | | |
| 17 | | | | | |
| 18 | | | | | |
| 19 | | | | | |
| 20 | | | | | |

FIGURE 8.5

# MAILING LOG

| | Name | Date Sent | Description of Mailing |
|---|---|---|---|
| 1 | | | |
| 2 | | | |
| 3 | | | |
| 4 | | | |
| 5 | | | |
| 6 | | | |
| 7 | | | |
| 8 | | | |
| 9 | | | |
| 10 | | | |
| 11 | | | |
| 12 | | | |
| 13 | | | |
| 14 | | | |
| 15 | | | |
| 16 | | | |
| 17 | | | |
| 18 | | | |
| 19 | | | |
| 20 | | | |

FIGURE 8.6

# PROMOTION PLANNER

### Date             Event

**QUARTER 1**

1 _____ _____

2 _____ _____

3 _____ _____

4 _____

### Date             Event

**QUARTER 2**

1 _____ _____

2 _____ _____

3 _____ _____

4 _____

### Date             Event

**QUARTER 3**

1 _____ _____

2 _____ _____

3 _____ _____

4 _____

### Date             Event

**QUARTER 4**

1 _____ _____

2 _____ _____

3 _____ _____

4 _____

FIGURE 8.7

# CLIENT GATHERING PLANNER

|  | | Date | Event |
|---|---|---|---|
| **QUARTER 1** | 1 | _____ | _____ |
| | 2 | _____ | _____ |
| | 3 | _____ | _____ |
| | 4 | _____ | _____ |

|  | | Date | Event |
|---|---|---|---|
| **QUARTER 2** | 1 | _____ | _____ |
| | 2 | _____ | _____ |
| | 3 | _____ | _____ |
| | 4 | _____ | _____ |

|  | | Date | Event |
|---|---|---|---|
| **QUARTER 3** | 1 | _____ | _____ |
| | 2 | _____ | _____ |
| | 3 | _____ | _____ |
| | 4 | _____ | _____ |

|  | | Date | Event |
|---|---|---|---|
| **QUARTER 4** | 1 | _____ | _____ |
| | 2 | _____ | _____ |
| | 3 | _____ | _____ |
| | 4 | _____ | _____ |

FIGURE 8.8

**Step 6:** Keep doing what works. Sounds basic, doesn't it? Yet we often get bored with what works long before our audience does. If it works, continue doing it. In this last chapter, you learned the story of the advisor who is still using today what worked for him when he started out in the business 30 years ago. Why? Because it *works*. The value of Gratitude Marketing™ ideas lies in using them consistently.

**Step 7**: If an idea stops working for you, rotate to another idea within a category (Personal, Fun, Seasonal, Mindful). What you will find is that as you implement the ideas and they work, you will be able to add new ideas to try out as your staff, resources, and increased revenues dictate. As you get accustomed to using this guide as a road map to Gratitude Marketing™ success, you'll be amazed at the additional ideas you can use to create some of your own strategies.

## LET'S REVIEW THE SEVEN STEPS TO IMPLEMENT YOUR GRATITUDE MARKETING™ STRATEGY:

1. Select a Gratitude Marketing™ idea from each of the four categories.

2. Ask yourself what it will take for you to implement them.

3. Record your commitments.

4. Schedule your activities on the Gratitude Marketing™ calendar.

5. Utilize the Gratitude Marketing™ templates to chart your progress.

6. Keep doing what works.

7. If an idea stops working, rotate to another idea in the same category.

In the spirit of offering a little lagniappe before we leave this chapter, I want to share with you another benefit of Gratitude Marketing™ that you may not have considered, and that is the positive word of mouth in your community and the referrals it generates. Imagine if every client were to refer someone to you. What impact would that have on your practice? The reality is some won't refer, but many more will. Clients readily provide referrals once they have experienced and seen the value of the work that you do. Implementing a client referral program is an efficient way to attract higher-quality clients.

**Implementing a client referral program is an efficient way to attract higher-quality clients.**

One evening, I arrived in town on a very late flight, and all I wanted to do was catch a taxi and get to the hotel as quickly as possible. To my surprise, I had a very engaging driver and we chatted throughout the ride. He shared some simple wisdom that I think applies to the idea of referrals. He said you have to bring something to the table in order to take something away. Translation: you have to create something invaluable for your clients in order for them to refer others to you.

Can you imagine a cost-effective and inexpensive way to receive a steady stream of quality referrals? What if you adopted a consistent, systematic approach to receiving referrals? And how much new businesses could this mean to you in your practice? A recent industry study showed that 80 percent of people who work with financial advisors say they would recommend their advisors to others. So if you want to raise your assets under management, the first people you should go to are those who are already your clients. They are, were, and always will be very important to your business.

Thinking back to when I first started in this business, my sales manager used to say, "Remember sales may keep you in the business, but referrals keep you in the sales." Over the years, in my travels across this great land, many successful financial advisors have shared some of their greatest referral ideas with me. I'd like to share them with you in the following pages.

The three reasons why clients do business with you are they like you, they trust you, and they respect you. How your clients feel about you and what they are prepared to tell others about you and your firm can greatly increase your revenue. Think about it. If you were to inherit $3 million today, how would you find an advisor? Would you look at an ad in the paper? Would you look at the yellow pages? No. You would probably ask a trusted friend or a business associate for a referral.

I have learned over the years that clients acquired through referrals are more profitable, invest more money, and invest more frequently. They also tend to be more loyal. The most successful advisors I know have positioned themselves as the resource, or the solution, for their clients. They provide the most relevant, timely, and high-quality answers to their clients' questions. Receiving a regular stream of referrals is an extra side benefit.

How do you turn on this perpetual referral machine?

**There are three strategies to cultivate referrals: (1) passive, (2) one at a time, and (3) proactive.**

There are three strategies to cultivate referrals: (1) passive, (2) one at a time, and (3) proactive. Here are four passive ideas that I've seen used, and all of them are various signs I've seen in financial advisors' offices.

1. Sign in the waiting area

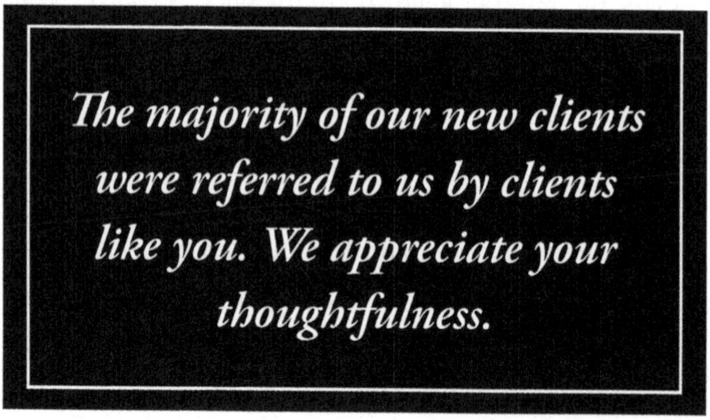

> *The majority of our new clients were referred to us by clients like you. We appreciate your thoughtfulness.*

FIGURE 8.9

2. Sign on the back of the office entrance door

> *Our practice continues to grow by referrals from our clients. Thank you for continuing to recommend us.*

FIGURE 8.10

3. The lobby cardholder

> *We appreciate your referrals. If you are pleased with our services, please give our card to a friend.*

FIGURE 8.11

4. Sign on the advisor's desk

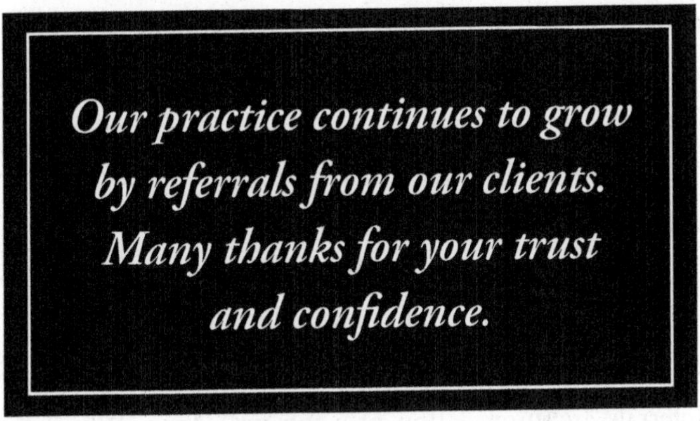

> *Our practice continues to grow by referrals from our clients. Many thanks for your trust and confidence.*

FIGURE 8.12

Before I proceed to strategies two and three, I must share one final passive idea with you. I received a calendar from an advisor friend at year's end. On the envelope flap he placed a two-inch, gold, circular sticker that read, "Oh by the way, I'm never too busy for your referrals." This advisor is tremendously successful because he never passes up an opportunity to ask for a referral. Referrals give you the opportunity to expand and open the channels of abundance in your practice.

In a recent industry study, it was reported that 67 percent of new clients and new revenue come from either a client referral or a center of influence referral, and yet less than one third of advisors have a formulized process for cultivating referrals. Make this a goal for this year. In the same way you listen for buying signals, pay attention to indicators of willingness to refer.

Strategies two and three involve identifying your ideal clients and then duplicating them one at a time.

To identify ideal clients, ask your current clients to recommend you to people like themselves. Use the four powerful words, *I need your help*. Ask them who else they believe could benefit from your services. What can your clients tell you about them? How would you approach them? How do your clients know these people? Successful financial advisors know that once clients have experienced and seen the value of the work they do, they will want to be helpful and give referrals, so be referable.

Continue to focus on this with your clients: underpromise and overperform. Do what you said you'd do and go the extra mile. Add so much value that your clients will want to refer you. Referrals are appreciation of a job well done. Why not choose to serve a limited number of the right clients and have a significant impact on their lives? From this day forward, think of your business as an infinite network of potential relationships. Make it a habit to just *ask for referrals*.

Finally, once you receive a referral, always remember to say thank you as all great gratitude marketers do. Send a handwritten note along with one of the following: a gift basket, a gift certificate for a dinner for two, or, perhaps, a magazine subscription. Offer to make a donation to the charity of the referrer's choice. Be sure to stay in touch with these clients on a regular basis and don't forget to send them a card on their birthdays or anniversaries, Thanksgiving, and Christmas. This is how you utilize some of the ideas I've already referred to in the book.

Here's one final idea on referrals, and it is strategy number three. At the end of your client's office visit, hand out three of your business cards. Remind your client that your business grows through word of mouth. Tell your client that you will call in seven days to get the names of those people to whom your client gave the cards. As Thomas Jefferson said, "Do you want to know who you are? Don't ask. Act. Action will delineate and define you."

My mission throughout this book has been simple: to offer perspectives and ideas that I developed over the years so that you may think in much bigger and broader ways about your practice. Years ago, a mentor shared with me some very helpful and important advice. He said that my mind-set would be positively or negatively impacted by the books I read and the people I associated with regularly. His advice was to simply write my own mind-set script in a positive and uplifting manner.

I found doing this has directly benefited my family, my clients, and me. Nurturing our mind-set daily is essential. It's an essential part of the Gratitude Marketing™ strategy. The caliber of information that we consistently put through our minds is what programs our mind on where to focus. A massive change will occur in your mind-set when you conceive of your business as interacting with people and enhancing their lives.

The successful financial advisors I've worked with consciously and deliberately control their mind-set. Through their thinking, they moved from being a salesperson to a trusted resource. Their practices evolved from chasing prospects to being pursued by them. What client wouldn't want to seek out and work with an advisor who fixes their pain and helps them with their needs?

There are numerous examples of the positive role mind-set plays in success. A musician must practice diligently to become a virtuoso. An athlete trains long hours before becoming a star performer. In that same vein, it takes practice to experience a meaningful mind-set adjustment. Begin by focusing on one moment, one hour, one day, one week, and one month at a time. Before you know it, you will have improved your mind-set.

There are four easy ways to script your mind-set:

1. Wake up earlier. It's really not as bad as it sounds. Allow yourself time to read something that will inspire you and influence your actions that day.

2. Script your day as if it had already happened. I know distractions will sometimes occur, but you will certainly accomplish more in a day if your day is well planned. Walt Disney was famous for this. He called it a script that your mind can follow. Your daily actions follow your mind.

3. In the morning, listen to motivational music while going to work. You can progress at your own pace and focus on the areas of your life that you want to improve now.

4. Ask yourself the same key question that Steve Jobs asked himself every day. Jobs, the founder of Apple, was a master of his own mind-set. He did one thing every morning to keep himself on track and focused. He looked into the mirror and asked himself, "If I die

tonight, will I be glad I did what I'm planning to do today?" What's your answer? If your answer is no, then you have a chance to change your plan and get busy exerting your own meaningful influence today.

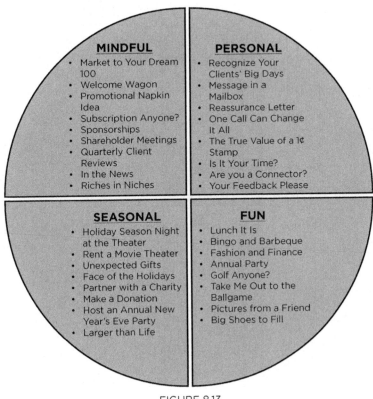

FIGURE 8.13

## MAKING GRATITUDE MARKETING™ WORK FOR YOU RECAP

Make the most of your opportunities; use Gratitude Marketing™ to be the advisor who impacts your clients' lives. Zig Ziglar said, "Feelings follow actions." So when you really don't feel like doing what needs to be done, do it, and then you will feel like doing it. Why wait? Challenge yourself today. As I've said, one step a day, and you will be 365 times better at year end. Once more, here are the steps:

1. Select a Gratitude Marketing™ idea from each of the four categories.

2. Ask yourself what it will take for you to implement them.

3. Record your commitments.

4. Schedule your activities on the Gratitude Marketing™ calendar.

5. Utilize the Gratitude Marketing™ templates to chart your progress.

6. Keep doing what works.

7. If an idea stops working, rotate to another idea in the same category.

# CHAPTER 9

# Finishing Strong

*Nothing is more honorable than a grateful heart.*

—SENECA

You may be wondering why every advisor doesn't use Gratitude Marketing™. Now, you know you can control how you build your business going forward through Gratitude Marketing™. Now, you know various ways in which you can stand up and get noticed in your community. You have discovered strategies to become memorable, top of mind, and to generate positive word of mouth for your business. Gratitude Marketing™ allows you to work smarter and let others help you leverage what you do while you stay top of mind with your clients and prospects. Having reached this point in the book, you are, I am convinced, committed to the idea that something has to change in your marketing. You have seen that Gratitude Marketing™ is different from ordinary marketing. It is creative and entertaining and helps you to stand out from the crowd.

A well-run Gratitude Marketing™ system will put you in control of your clients' business consistently as change occurs and their need for your services arises or increases. The more you implement Gratitude Marketing™, the easier it will become. So now I invite you to write your own check.

| | | 1027 |
|---|---|---|
| | | DATE |
| PAY TO THE ORDER OF | | $ |
| | DOLLARS | |
| FOR | | |

⑈22222222⑈ ⑇ 000 ⑈⑈⑈ 555⑈⑈ ⑈027

FIGURE 9.1

By how much would you like to grow your business, and what will that do to your bottom line? Will Rogers said, "If you want to be successful, it's just this simple. Know what you are doing, love what you are doing, and believe in what you are doing."

**A well-run Gratitude Marketing™ system will put you in control of your clients' business consistently as change occurs and their need for your services arises or increases.**

Through the sharing of proven ideas, this book addresses two of the largest problems in our business today: asset retention and succession planning. It provides you with solutions to each problem. The strategies I offer rely on your effective application of not just one strategy but, rather, the development of a long-term, deliberate relationship, nurturing and building a plan that employs a number of ideas simultaneously, not sequentially. The primary promise I make to you is that, with these concepts, you will expand your business through authentic connections with your clients.

Years ago, I read an interview with Fran Tarkenton, the former Minnesota Vikings quarterback. As successful as he was as a quarterback, he has enjoyed even greater success as a business owner, having started and sold several businesses. When asked what the one key to success was, his response was remarkably simple. He said that whether it was a customer, a supplier, or an employee, "I try to do whatever it takes to make their lives better." He was a master at Gratitude Marketing™, and you can be too.

Gratitude Marketing™ allows you to genuinely express who you are to your clients. Research on sales has confirmed over and over again that who you have made yourself out to be in the minds of your clients or prospects is far more influential than what you say. What you decide to do today is important because you are exchanging a day of your life for it.

Let me illustrate with the following perspective on time. Over the years, I've seen many variations of this poem by an unknown author. It's titled "Time."

*Imagine there is a bank account that credits your account each morning with $86,400. It carries over no balance from day to day.*

*Every evening the bank deletes whatever part of the balance you failed to use during the day. What would you do? Draw out every cent, of course.*

*Each of us has such a bank. Its name is TIME.*

*Every morning, it credits you with 86,400 seconds.*

*Every night it writes off as lost whatever of this you have failed to invest to a good purpose.*

*It carries over no balance. It allows no overdraft. Each day it opens a new account for you. Each night it burns the remains of the day.*

*If you fail to use the day's deposits, the loss is yours. There is no drawing against "tomorrow."*

*You must live in the present on today's deposits. Invest it so as to get from it the utmost in health, happiness, and success! The clock is running! Make the most of today.*

Earlier, I mentioned that I began this book asking myself what I wish I had known when I was starting out in this business. I remember two things in particular about that time: (1) the Dow was at 776, not at the 17,000+ level it is as I write today, and (2) on my desk by my phone I had taped the Calvin Coolidge quote on persistence—more on that in a moment. Ever since then I have had a passion for learning how to maintain peak performance and share the results with financial advisors I work with. What I have learned is that it is possible to maintain a regular and consistent level of peak performance if you employ the following four keys:

**P** — persistence

**E** — enthusiasm

**A** — attitude

**K** — kindness

Let's break each of these down.

> **Persistence:** We all get knocked down from time to time. These are the times you need to *give* of yourself a little bit more. The marathon runner hits a wall. The boxer hits the mat. Many times, the problems or challenges we face force us to grow and become more capable. Those who persist in spite of the obstacles they encounter consistently prevail. They reach ahead to achieve their vision of the future. Calvin Coolidge said, "Nothing in this world can take the place of persistence. Talent will not; nothing is more common than unsuccessful men with talent. Genius will not; unrewarded genius is almost a proverb. And education will not; the world is full of educated derelicts. Persistence and determination alone are omnipotent."

**Enthusiasm:** It's been said that nothing great was ever achieved without enthusiasm. Enthusiasm is that feeling, emotion, or power within that drives you to take action. Those with enthusiasm display a special eagerness or zeal to achieve their goals. They throw everything they have into a project, become passionate, and set themselves apart. Norman Vincent Peale wrote, "There is real magic in enthusiasm. It spells the difference between mediocrity and its accomplishment."

**Attitude:** You can quickly identify peak performers by their attitude. It is the little difference that makes a big difference. People can feel your attitude. Most gravitate toward those who exhibit a positive and uplifting attitude. We all have the ability each day to *choose* a positive attitude. According to Zig Ziglar, your attitude, not your aptitude, will determine your altitude.

**Kindness: This is the universal language that connects all people. It may sometimes be unexpected, but it is always welcome. Likewise, gratitude is another thing that is often unexpected but never unwelcomed.**

**Kindness:** This is the universal language that connects all people. It may sometimes be unexpected, but it is always welcome, as gratitude marketers have learned. "Constant kindness can accomplish much. As the sun makes ice melt, kindness causes misunderstanding, mistrust, and hostility to evaporate." That is an Albert Schweitzer quote.

Peak performers are strategists who continue to learn, continue to strive, and continue to move forward one day at a time. Their secret is simple: Peak performers have learned how to celebrate the past, nurture the future, and delight in each moment. Once financial advisors realize they are the creators of all the experiences, situations, problems, and successes going on in their lives and they can create all that differently, they realign the direction in which they want their actions to go. One of the most important words in business is *clarity*. As we wind down our journey together, ask yourself what you are trying to do and why you are trying to do it.

There are six reasons for implementing Gratitude Marketing™.

1. When your clients experience kindness and generosity from your business, it makes them want to support you, it helps you cultivate referrals, it builds trust, and it makes people feel good about themselves and their decisions.

2. Giving to others is the greatest gift you can give yourself. Studies show that when you help others, you release additional endorphins into your system, producing what is called the "helper's high."

3. The cost of obtaining new customers is high—about seven times the cost of keeping existing customers. It is a lot cheaper to retain than acquire. Gratitude Marketing™ allows you to employ new methods to extend existing relationships.

4. The number-one asset your business has is your client relationship. The deeper and stronger that relationship is, the more value your practice will have. How many of

you have regular systems in place to contact your clients? Gratitude Marketing™ will give you those systems.

5. A client relationship can become more valuable if you commit to regular, consistent, meaningful communication. I encourage you to test your communication and urge you to tabulate and monitor your results. Gratitude is one thing that is often unexpected but never unwelcomed.

6. It's a great exit strategy. Your company will sell for more if you institute predictable systems such as Gratitude Marketing™. It's the most reliable route to increasing your return income in your business, which, ultimately, determines your company's value. Gratitude Marketing™ will help you cultivate unique, long-lasting relationships with your clients.

In his *Southwest* magazine interview, computer magnate Michael Dell explained that he believed his company would continue to be successful because of its unique relationship with its customers. He said, "As long as we continue to pay heed to what our clients tell us they want and deliver products and services that are meaningful to them and that deliver superior value, we will continue to be successful." Gratitude Marketing™ helps *you* do this. Successful financial advisors are constantly seeking knowledge that will improve their lives and their practice. We are all a measure of our habits. Studying and adapting the habits of successful financial advisors will help you be more profitable in business and happier in life.

As I write this chapter, I am filled with an enormous amount of gratitude. Just last week, my wife and I welcomed our first granddaughter into the world. As all children are, Anna is a blessing, bringing new life, hope, and energy to our family. She is another reminder to me of how much we have to be thankful for and why I must continue on my path to devote my life to helping others grow and reach their potential. I believe, as Einstein did, that it is every man's obligation to put back into the world at least the equivalent of what he takes out. It really is amazing what happens when you recognize the importance of the opportunities ahead of you, accept responsibility for your future, and take positive action.

Now that you've experienced the numerous ideas used by successful financial advisors, you leave this book not just as a marketer but as a gratitude marketer. As Woodrow Wilson said, "I not only use all the brains I have but all that I can borrow." You are borrowing the proven wisdom of successful advisors. Adopting the Gratitude Marketing™ mind-set works.

In writing this book, I have developed a stronger sense of gratitude for those who have had an impact on my life through their willingness to teach, mentor, and share with me. It has also brought back to me just how significantly these ideas and this mind-set have influenced my career in ways I had forgotten. It has deepened my commitment to help other financial advisors build robust, stable, sustainable practices anchored by strong values and morals.

Mark Twain believed that, in 20 years from now, you will be more disappointed by the things you didn't do than by the ones you did. So throw off the bowline, sail away from the safe harbor, catch the trade winds in your sails, explore, dream, and discover. The time to implement is now. The fantastic thing about life is that, every day, you have the freedom to decide whether you want the rest of your years to be the best of your years.

This doesn't happen by chance but by your choice. Today my challenge to you is to revise and rethink how you've been building your practice. Embrace Gratitude Marketing™ at this moment, and commit to yourself to take these ideas and implement them *now*. Today is where tomorrow's success lies. You have been gracious enough to allow me to occupy some of your precious time. For that, I'd like to express my gratitude for allowing me to share these proven ideas with you. I wish you much success in their implementation.

Let me leave you with two more quotes. According to Thomas Jefferson, "wisdom is knowing what to do next, skill is knowing how to do it, but virtue is actually doing it." You now *know* how to become a successful gratitude marketer; all you have to do is *implement*. T. S. Elliot wrote, "Only those who will risk going too far can possibly find out how far they can go." How significant will your impact be? As financial advisors, we have been entrusted with a tremendous responsibility. True significance in our business comes by not only knowing what to do for our clients but in actually doing it. The value of the ideas in this book is in using them. To be a great gratitude marketer, you have to step out of the industry. You can't just stay tunnel-focused in our business. You have to look at every industry. When you see a nice marketing approach in another company, you have to ask how you can apply it to your practice.

The other day, I visited a college to speak to MBA students. As I thought about what I was going to say and what value I was going to bring to these students, I started breaking my career down into three chapters. Chapter 1 was when I was a stockbroker, my dream job out of college. And what I learned in that chapter of my career was about time. I found out very quickly that you can dial a phone 300 times a day, and I didn't want to do that forever. This knowledge forced me to be creative, and that was the point where I stepped out of my comfort zone and started speaking to groups. Chapter 2 was the period I spent on the wholesale side of the business. I realized from observing some of the older advisors who mentored me that they always had a way of differentiating themselves. One guy had a really nice handkerchief that he put in his suits. He was always dressed to the nines with his nice handkerchief. I decided then and there to do two things to differentiate myself in the business. I was going to be the best-dressed wholesaler out there. And I vowed not to be a professional visitor but, rather, a professional resource who added value to each financial advisor he worked with. A professional visitor is somebody who goes around to offices and wastes the advisors' time and never really gets down to the work of helping them build their business. Before I went out on visits in any given week, I would create manila folders for each advisor I called on. Based on my previous meetings with the advisor and his or her particular needs, I would put into that folder everything that I wanted to cover. Once I'd reached into my bag and pulled out that folder, the advisor suddenly realized it was time to do business. It was a differentiating factor, and it still works today.

The third chapter in my career came when I realized that I had something to share with others in our industry: my passion for Gratitude Marketing™. And so I reinvented myself. I'm now connecting advisors, sharing their strategies for Gratitude Marketing™, and reaching a broader market. It's had a big impact not only on my life but on the lives of many others as well.

If you can put your head on your pillow at night knowing you have had a positive impact on peoples' lives and you have created clients for life, you will have a lot to be grateful for, too. To get us started working together, let me ask you one question: What was the most significant piece of advice that anyone has given you in your business, and how do you apply that advice to your business? Submit your ideas to me at Mike@gratitudemarketingbook.com.

The value of the ideas in this book lies in sharing them. What groups, organizations, or companies do you know that would benefit from the many ideas in this book? What events do you know of that need an impactful speaker? I have just scratched the surface of ideas I can provide to those who are serious about building their business.

If you would like to learn more about Gratitude Marketing™ in general or would like more information on implementing the ideas contained in this book, please connect with me by visiting gratitudemarketingbook.com. Once there, you can find out how you are doing currently concerning Gratitude Marketing™ by answering the questions on the Gratitude Marketing™ Assessment. Or even better, e-mail me directly at Mike@gratitudemarketingbook.com. I look forward to sharing everything I know to help you become the best gratitude marketer in the business—*now*.

*Destiny is not a matter of chance, but a matter of choice. It is not a thing to be waited for but is a thing to be achieved.*

—WILLIAM JENNINGS BRYAN

# ACKNOWLEDGMENTS

As Albert Schweitzer, winner of the 1952 Nobel Peace Prize, said, "At times, our own light goes out and is rekindled by a spark from another person. Each of us has cause to think with deep gratitude of those who have lighted the flame within us."

Of course there are many who deserve my gratitude and recognition for all their enthusiastic contributions over the years. I must begin with my parents. They constantly offered me encouragement and taught me the importance of values and the true meaning of love. My mother-in-law was heaven-sent, and her legacy lives on in our hearts.

I have had the great privilege to be with and work with so many great friends, mentors, coaches, colleagues, and advisors who, in their own way, are a unique part of this book. A special thanks goes out to the Advantage team. My editor is a tremendous professional. Her ability to pinpoint the objectives and stay focused and provide excellent insights has been of great value.

Finally, my deepest gratitude goes to my wife, children, grandchildren, sister, brother, and extended family for their support and inspiration to make today and every day extraordinary. You are all awesome.

# ABOUT THE AUTHOR

Michael F. Sciortino Sr. is founder and CEO of Gratitude Marketing™, a firm specializing in helping advisors grow their practices through carefully nurturing long-term relationships. Mike possesses a rare perspective and combination of practical marketing applications in retail, wholesale, traditional, and alternative investments. He has discovered how implementing a Gratitude Marketing™ system in the practices of financial advisors can increase client retention, increase referrals, increase revenues, and bridge the gap to the next generation. He began his career in 1983 as an account executive with E. F. Hutton, where he led the office in opening new account relationships. Following that position, Mike transitioned into wholesaling with Colonial Investments and Pilgrim Funds, where he was recognized for leading the most-improved sales team. He then went on to spend 13 years as regional VP with Oppenheimer Funds. While at Oppenheimer, Mike conducted seminars to assist financial advisors in building their practices, and his territories surpassed the company's growth rate every year. Most recently, Mike served as executive vice president and head of distribution for an RIA. Mike was responsible for directing the company's overall marketing and sales strategy by broadening the relationships between the company and the financial advisors they work with.

Mike is a recipient of the Order of St. Louis IX medallion presented by the archdiocese of New Orleans, honoring those members of the laity who have made outstanding contributions. Mike is a graduate of the University of New Orleans with a bachelor of science degree in finance.

CPSIA information can be obtained at www.ICGtesting.com
Printed in the USA
BVOW06*0819271015

424338BV00013B/153/P